The Manager's Diary II

Step Up Before Your Employees Step Down

Cameron Morrissey

Copyright © 2015 Cameron Morrissey

All rights reserved.

ISBN-10: 1515333167
ISBN-13: 978-1515333166

For Jonathan & Olivia

You are the brightest parts of my day

TABLE OF CONTENTS

Preface... *vii*
Introduction... *ix*

Hiding in Plain Sight:
Obvious Things We're Too Busy to Notice

Deadlines are Your Lifelines...	3
Stay Away from Debbie Downers.....................................	4
Checklists Aren't Just for Rocket Launches.......................	6
One of My Best Leadership Tips.......................................	8
Recovering Quickly Speeds Up Success............................	11
Take the Next Step..	12
Easier to be Honest...	15
Do the Little Things Right..	17
It Gets Harder Before It Gets Easier.................................	19
Never as Bad as it Looks, and Never as Good Either.......	21
Assume There is Always a Better Way..............................	23
Solutions are Useless if not Acted Upon..........................	25
The Right Steps Only Matter If You Get The Right Results....	27
Anybody Can be a Skeptic, Leaders Create Solutions.....	29
Have No Enemies...	31

The Staff:
Managing For Success

Don't Even Think About Reading This.............................	37
Be a Voyeur Manager...	38
Over-Communicate or You Risk Not Communicating Enough......	40
Why Fun is Important to any Team..................................	42
Find the Engine of Action...	44
You are the Shock Absorber...	46
Keep People Engaged and Excited...................................	48
Tackle Unnecessary Obstacles...	50
Believe in the Unbelievable..	51

Feed Random Employee Passions.. 53
Leverage Strengths and Weaknesses................................... 55
Manage Your Good News Delivery...................................... 56
Jump Under the Bus.. 58
Make all of the Negative Changes at Once............................. 60
Failure Is Not An Option.. 62
Lay the Foundation for Success.. 64
Own the Stories... 66
Little Gestures Go a Long Way... 67
Master the Message (Part 1 - Bad News).............................. 69
Master the Message (Part 2 – Good News)............................ 71
Reach 10% and Effect 10% More....................................... 73

Great Talent:
Hard To Find & Tough To Develop

Don't Be Your Own Worst Enemy When Hiring...................... 79
Have You Identified Your Successor.................................... 81
Learn From the Routine... 83
Let Your Staff Vote on Stuff.. 84
Leverage the New Hires for Excitement................................ 86

Yourself:
If You Can't Mange Yourself, You're In Trouble

It Only Takes Two Seconds to be a Better Leader................... 93
Great Leaders Laugh at Work.. 94
Fresh Air for Fresh Ideas.. 96
How to Be a Know It All at Work....................................... 98
Get in the Habit of Turning Off Your Smartphone.................. 100
Are You an Ambidextrous Leader...................................... 102
Can't Play Until You've Eaten Your Vegetables..................... 104
The Enemy of Management: The Grey Area......................... 106
The Big Picture is for Perspective not Excuses...................... 108
Don't Be So Smart You're Stupid – Part 1............................ 110
Don't Be So Smart You're Stupid – Part 2............................ 112
What is Your Worst Habit.. 114
Staffs Judge on Every Decision You Make........................... 116

Rethink Metrics... 117
Should Do versus Need to Do... 119
Don't Let a Detail Derail a Purpose................................. 121
Fall in Love with Your Problems...................................... 123
Being Busy Makes Things Easier...................................... 125
The Pathway to Leadership... 127
Quick Draws Aim Poorly.. 129
You Should Not Heed All Advice.................................... 130
Find a Mentor When Reaching for the Stars................. 132
Your Business and Career Runs on Promises................. 134
One Battle at a Time... 136
What is Your Mission or Basic Values............................ 138
What Can YOU Work On.. 140
What Got You Here, Won't Get You There................. 141
Repair Relationships.. 143
Rearrange Your Day for Maximum Effectiveness......... 144
Your Job is to Deal with the Non-Ideal Situations....... 147
Be the Change You Want To See.................................... 149
Don't Tell Me, Show Me Instead..................................... 151
Relax When Looking at the Huge Work in Front of You........ 152
See What You Need to on an Excel Spreadsheet.......... 154
Work with What You Have, Don't Wait For "Pie in the Sky"........ 156
Do You Have The Right People on Your Team?........... 158
Keep Checking Your Map... 160
Why I Hate PowerPoint and What to Learn From It... 162
The Fish Stinks From the Head....................................... 164
Management is Easy, Just Always be Right................... 166
New Thinking on Dressing for Success.......................... 167
Don't Just See What YOU Want to See......................... 169

Projects:
When All Eyes Are Watching

Plan to Fail.. 175
The First Feedback Can Be the Most Important......... 177
Flip-flopping Isn't Always Bad... 179
Always Toughest Near the Mountaintop....................... 181
Don't Fall in Love with Your Plan.................................. 183
The Goal Isn't a Field Goal.. 184
Overinvest in Early Wins.. 186

Peers:
You're a Player Not Just a Coach

Beware of the Agreement Monster.................................... 193
Take Care of Those Who Take Care of You........................ 195
Fresh Ideas from the Un-involved..................................... 197
How to Turn Defeat into Victory....................................... 199
Feeling Down or Un-empowered? Go Next Door.................. 201
Be the Focused and Calming Influence.............................. 202
A Rising Tide Raises All Boats... 204

The Customer:
The Reason You Have a Job

Find Competitive Advantage Anywhere You Can................. 209
Create Value for Sustained Success................................... 211
Focus on Things That Won't Change.................................. 214

Appendix I
Top Leadership & Management Quotes

Quotes #101-#200.. 217

Epilogue... *225*

Preface

Five years ago when I started on this journey I never thought I'd be writing my third book. I just set out to chronicle and share the lessons I was learning (usually the hard way) while going through my career in management. It turns out that the principles and practices of leadership and management are subjects of enormous depth, so new material and new lessons were always presenting themselves.

This book continues the tradition of presenting managers and leaders with practical material that came about in the real world, not in any sort of academic setting. I have added more content this time around and quickened the pace of writing to accommodate our fast paced work environments. One thing that remains the same, however, is the focus on putting the knowledge into practice as it is only through action that we can affect change on our environments.

Introduction

Five minutes a day. That's all it takes to grow your leadership style and change the course of your career. You just need to find the right resource. This book is intentionally set up into "bite-sized" segments to make it as sensitive to your time demands as possible and to keep you hyper-focused on the content. One chapter every work day and one Lesson Assignment every work day. Like compounding interest, the effect at the end of the time period will be much greater than the sum of its parts.

The challenge is to put the content and the Lesson Assignments into practice immediately. Knowledge is useless if it is not applied, so I encourage you to be diligent in making every attempt to put the subject matter into use in your organization right away. This is where you will receive your value.

How you navigate through the book; bouncing between topics of interest, starting at the beginning and working straight through, or bouncing between sections is up to you. You may be surprised at some of the topics that impact you, whether it be because we simply don't think of them very often, or we have differing points of view. For that reason you should plan to touch on every subject to get the most from your experience.

Lastly I want to make sure that you stay focused on enjoying the journey. Some of these topics are fun and some of them are anything but fun. Try to focus on your growth as a leader and you'll find it easier to push through the tougher stretches. I wish you nothing but the best on this journey. Enjoy!

Hiding in Plain Sight:

Obvious Things We're Too Busy to Notice

The Manager's Diary II

Deadlines are Your Lifelines

"You don't need more time, you just need to decide" ~Seth Godin

"Be clear about your goal but be flexible about the process of achieving it." ~ Brian Tracy

· · · · ·

A fantastic habit to work on is associating deadlines with every single one of the items you assign your staff, are assigned yourself in meetings, or quite frankly any task you assign yourself. The first "grey area" with any task is how important it is. Should it be prioritized ahead of other tasks? Can it wait until later? Do I want to do it, etc? The deadline for completion is one of the central parts of that discussion. This cuts down on any miscommunication you may have with your staff on timing. Some of the other benefits of deadlines are:

- **Begins clarifying and defining outcomes** – Taking away those "grey areas" is one of the most important things we do in management. By defining the timeframe, you begin the discussion of goals and measurements.
- **Let's people adjust their plans** – I believe this is one of the most profound benefits. If you are clear about your deadlines, your staff can ask for clarification on where the item fits in with other deadlines, or even better, can arrange their work themselves (a great way to increase empowerment).

- **Puts a sense of urgency in place** – This is one of the most commonly cited reasons for instituting deadlines, and it can definitely accomplish a sense of urgency (which in theory is supposed to make people work harder). However, I think that the benefits above are even more beneficial to the long-run effectiveness of your staff.

Of course, the next step to conveying what your deadline is on a task is asking for feedback on whether there are any roadblocks to it. And it is important that you are *open* to that feedback. One of the first failings of deadlines can be that they are unreasonable and there is no openness to assist with how to deal with any anticipated conflicts. If there is no "buy-in" to the deadline it instantly turns useless. So with that one warning I bid you to get started with conveying deadlines.

LESSON ASSIGNMENT: Assigning deadlines isn't necessarily the problem, it is setting one that people can buy into. As with all things this will take practice. Start with a goal of assigning a deadline to everything, but a side goal to ask the person for their feedback on whether the deadline is realistic. Please have this underway no later than today. :-)

Stay Away from Debbie Downers

"I will listen to anyone's convictions, but please keep your doubts to yourself."
~Goethe

"Negativity breeds negativity. The wise focus on the positive in every person and every situation." ~Philip Arnold

Step Up Before Your Employees Step Down

· · · · ·

Feedback is essential, but managing who you get it from and who you listen to is just as essential. Getting feedback about your initiatives, ideas, and the overall state of the business from those who are consistently negative and cynical can not only be demoralizing, but also detrimental to your career ambitions by paralyzing your inclination to take action.

While it is important to have a "foil" or "devil's advocate" to filter your thoughts and ideas to make them better and increase clarity, we need to steer clear of those who would be executioners of ideas. "Debbie Downers" are inclined to be that way for a few reasons:

- **Poor vision** – Those who are consistently negative have a tendency to only be able to see things from a limited viewpoint, usually their own. Without the ability to see past the first obstacle to what lies beyond, they are stuck *only* seeing the obstacles which becomes the focus of the feedback they provide to you.
- **Poorly informed** – Negativity also comes from not having all of the facts, or only getting "facts" from likewise negatively skewed individuals. This lack of impartial information on their part limits positivity and compounds negativity.
- **Risk Averse** – Partly because of the above two points, "Debbie Downers" are usually not interested in changes to the status quo as they do not see the potential for upside. They only see extra work, problems, and eventually just wasted time.
- **Insecure** – The worst thing for insecure or lazy people is to see a secure person push forward, put a bunch of ideas/initiatives into motion and create success. It justifies their inaction by holding you back.
- **"Vampires"** – A term used by HR in leadership development classes at a former company of mine. Some people just thrive on gossip and finding everything wrong. It's easier to shoot down ideas than come up with ideas on your own, or even more so, persevering through the inevitable challenges of

putting something new in place or maintaining a positive attitude through troubles.

You are not looking to surround yourself with "Yes" men or women, but on the other hand, be careful of being surrounded by "No" men and women as well. Evaluate those whom you receive feedback from and make sure you aren't getting feedback that always represents "the glass is half empty" mentality. If you don't you are unnecessarily handicapping yourself.

LESSON ASSIGNMENT: Make a list of three people that are hugely positive around the office and a list of three people who are hugely negative. Now this week look to swap some of your time with the one group for the other. Some may be natural time swaps (asking for an opinion) and some may not (sitting with them in the lunchroom).

Checklists Aren't Just for Rocket Launches

"One of the most important tasks of a manager is to eliminate his people's excuses for failure." ~Robert Townsend

"Almost all quality improvement comes via simplification of design, manufacturing... layout, processes, and procedures." ~Tom Peters

. . . . .

Have you been having trouble with procedural compliance or with errors? Do you have a complicated or long process? Need a way to get newly hired employees "on the ground" and working right away? Checklists may be the answer for you.

Checklists have a number of benefits, but chief among them is that they break down tasks into simple steps and by doing so, builds confidence for the employee. They also ensure uniform procedural compliance and a reduction of errors (essential in your most important tasks). Sounds great right? So why don't more people use them then? Well they have a number of detractions as well: Chief among them, they can make tasks tedious and they all but eliminate creativity. This can make a checklist heavy job boring and demoralizing for the employee.

So what to do? Well it obviously depends on your workplace and the type of work that your staff does, but to the extent that you feel appropriate, what I recommend is targeted and temporary checklists:

- **Targeted #1 - The most important and critical tasks** – Areas where mistakes simply cannot be tolerated due to financial implications or customer support issues for example may benefit from a checklist. Remember, we're looking for just the most critical tasks or procedures.
- **Targeted #2 - Tasks where creativity isn't needed** – Since by their very nature checklists eliminate the ability for modification or customization, creative tasks should have at most "guidelines" to ensure that the mind of the employee is free to explore.
- **Temporary #1 – Training/New Procedure Roll-out** – Always a nice tool for the new hire to give them confidence and as a reference. Just remember that excessive use of checklists can become a crutch, so make sure you have a target date for letting them work "without a net".
- **Temporary #2 - Areas that have cropped up as a problem** – Sometimes everyone just needs a reminder on the proper way to handle things, or for whatever reason there is a need to focus on a particular task. When that occurs it is often beneficial to work with and provide a checklist. Again, you can't focus on everything, so these may be temporary as the focus/need shifts, but this will ensure that everyone is on the same page.

Checklists by their design are inflexible, which is often a very good thing. If you haven't worked with them in your operation, there may be an opportunity to gain some benefit. On the flip side, if you operation is heavily dependent on checklists your employees may benefit and get a sense of empowerment from eliminating some of the unnecessary checklists.

LESSON ASSIGNMENT: Ask yourself what a few of your biggest procedural problem areas are? Put together a checklist for the one where it seems most appropriate. It can be temporary or permanent, it could be up on the whiteboard or handed out. The key is for you to see what a checklist can do in your operation and you can make that decision later.

One of My Best Leadership Tips

"I've been blessed to find people who are smarter than I am, and they help me to execute the vision I have." ~Russell Simmons

"No one who achieves success does so without acknowledging the help of others. The wise acknowledge this help with gratitude." ~Unknown

. . . . .

Do you want to accomplish more? Do you want to do it quicker? Do you want to foster collaboration? Then practice consciously asking for help at least once a day. You will be *amazed* at the results.

Step Up Before Your Employees Step Down

In today's business environment we simply do not ask for help nearly enough. We may ask for it occasionally, but we almost always err on the side of not asking for help. This leaves us struggling in areas of weakness, spending less time in areas of strength, and making mistakes that could have been avoided. The reasons are relatively obvious:

- **We will show how much we don't know** – Our pride gets the better of us so we struggle to learn something that may have limited value later on. We make mistakes others have made before, and we create a substandard result because of it. All this so that we can manage our image and save ourselves the potential embarrassment.
- **We will get turned down for assistance** – The classic fear of rejection scenario that ignores that you will be successful a certain percentage of the time. Focus on the wins, not the losses.
- **We don't want to make more work for others** - There is the fear of being a burden on others, which neglects the fact that you can return the favor of time and expertise.
- **We prefer to count on our own efforts and knowledge** – This confused sense of "ownership" is just an excuse for our unwillingness to listen to others or our poorly developed ability to manage the work of others.

However, when we lean on the expertise and wisdom of the entire organization we create synergies and this creates amazing results for the organization:

- *Better Products and Results* – Sharing the wisdom and experience to get it right the first time.
- *Greater Employee Engagement* – Subject matter experts will often come from your staff.
- *Quicker Learning Curves* – No need to cut a new path when someone else has already blazed a trail before.

- *Greater Empowerment* – By letting people run with areas they are comfortable with, you can confidently let them take charge.
- *Greater Collaboration* – The very nature of asking for help builds greater collaboration between the parties that wouldn't have existed before.
- *More Time, not Less Time* – Less miscommunication, more time in your areas of strength, less time in your weak areas. It's Economics 101 and it all creates more time for you to accomplish even more.

Helping each other can easily turn contagious. As you work on this and see it grow into larger functional areas, you can look back on it and see that you were the person who helped create greater and greater collaboration within your organization.

LESSON ASSIGNMENT: Start by offering your assistance where you see it could be used. Make a goal of offering your assistance to someone at least once per day. Once you have had some takers on your offer then begin asking for assistance with some *small* things. From there you can move onto further and further collaboration with ever larger things.

Recovering Quickly Speeds Up Success

"Sometimes when you innovate, you make mistakes. It is best to admit them quickly, and get on with improving your other innovations." ~Steve Jobs

"Failure is a prerequisite for great success. If you want to succeed faster, double your rate of failure." ~Brian Tracy

. . . . .

We talk a lot about learning from failure and how failure is a key to eventual success, but what I wanted to speak briefly about is the importance of increasing the speed with which we recover from failure. While we must take some time to reflect on our mistakes, it is also beneficial to "get back on the horse you fell off of" as quickly as possible. You have to keep moving toward your goal. Taking action to better your circumstances is one of the keys to happiness, and in this case, turns a negative situation back towards the positive. The quicker we do that the better.

So because I find it easier to take action when I have step-by-step instructions to follow, I offer the following when you make a mistake:

- **Acknowledge the mistake** – The quicker you acknowledge that there was something that could have done to prevent what happened, the better for everyone. It is important to not deflect blame, but to acknowledge who and what was really responsible.
- **Determine what went wrong** – Make sure you understand what went wrong. I know this seems simplistic, but what went

wrong on the surface is often caused by something under the surface. With that said, be careful not to overanalyze and get stuck in the "paralysis by analysis" trap.
- **Find a solution** – How can you fix what went wrong? Do a quick brainstorming where you don't take into account how much time, effort and resources go into the solution (this opens the door to potentially new solutions). Once you have your list, *then* evaluate ease of implementation and how well each one will solves the issue.
- **Get back going** – Put the fix into place and get going toward success!

Don't dwell on your mistakes, tackle them head on with passion. If you speed up your resolution of mistakes, you speed up your rate of failure and therefore get to success faster.

LESSON ASSIGNMENT: Write out the above steps on a piece of paper. Make 10 copies and keep these copies in your desk. The next time you make a decent sized mistake or see a failure, take out one of the pieces of paper and get to work.

Take the Next Step

"It's never crowded along the extra mile" ~Wayne Dyer

"Go as far as you can see; when you get there, you'll be able to see farther." ~J. P. Morgan

Step Up Before Your Employees Step Down

· · · · ·

Going one step past the problem can often be the most important thing you do in dealing with problem resolution. Too often we are so focused on quickly taking care of the issue at hand that we never address the root of the problem. That "root" is almost always found after spending some time and energy digging.

- We find a substitute product for a customer, but never find out why our inventory didn't have enough of the product they originally wanted.
- We fix the customer's problem, but never pass it along to development so that they can write a bug fix.
- We open the creaky front door in every weird way imaginable to minimize the noise instead of getting some WD-40 for the hinges.

This leads to a recurring problem and wasted time and energy. In the most shortsighted organizations this leads to the opposite of economies of scale, they have larger staffs that are increasingly less efficient as they struggle to handle greater complexity and never actually address the root of the problems that pop up as they get larger.

On the flip side, if you as the leader of your department start tackling the root of the problems, you find your staff with more and more time to add value to the organization. The best departments often get smaller as they get better at doing their work, or they stay the same size but are entrusted with more responsibility. Some of the key next step questions these departments ask:

- **What caused this to happen?** After I fix *this*, I need to fix *that*. I need to either address it myself or get another stakeholder to address it.

- **How can we do this better next time?** Could the process be made quicker, or could we add things at little cost in expense and time to make it better.
- **Then they ask these questions again** – Often the cause of a problem has its root in another issue, which has its root in another issue, etc. Or in the case of improvement, there is almost always another one that can be made after you complete the first one.

Almost any question leads to a "next step". Once you open one door, you often find many more doors to open. Yes, I just increased the number of problems you have (sorry), but we are in our roles to continuously improve operations. One of the most directed ways to do that is to solve problems or issues that already exist. So ask the next question, look one step further in the process, and ensure you are addressing the root of the problem. Over time, you'll see that this investment not only saves you time, but increases your effectiveness.

LESSON ASSIGNMENT: Think back to the last five problems you solved. Did you solve the root cause or did you just make the problem go away? Start with one of these instances and make an attempt to fix the root cause. It may be training, it may be changing a process, whatever it is, fix it once and for all.

Easier to be Honest

"If a reporter asked if you and Hardin were friends, I'd say "good friends". If they asked if you were good friends, I'd say "lifelong friends". Give them no place to go, nothing to report. No story. I mean, it's no sense in defusing a bomb after it's already.....it's already gone off." ~Jack Ryan – A Clear and Present Danger

"Confidence... thrives on honesty, on honor, on the sacredness of obligations, on faithful protection and on unselfish performance. Without them it cannot live." ~Franklin D. Roosevelt

. . . . .

Listen, I won't go into a big long speech about it because most of us should already know it, but let me give you a few reasons why it is so much *easier* to just be honest and insist on honesty in your operation. Hopefully you can use these to either convince a counterpart or give yourself some extra motivation to carry on:

- **Not a relaxing massage** – It takes a lot of mental effort to "massage" the truth, which is really just telling white lies. You need to be creative, but at the same time careful, and that balance takes a *huge* amount of mental aerobics. This mental effort could be better spent working on departmental excellence.
- **Smoke and mirrors** – Dishonesty is most rampant when hiding mistakes or poor results, yet these are the things that should be looked at *most*. Our failures are our best instructors, so if you hide them, you're just extending the amount of time you're going to be "in school."

- **Don't worry about memory lapse** – What you said to whom and when you said it gets more and more and more complicated and time consuming as the lie ages. "Lies beget lies" is a very true statement that just adds more complication to things. The fear of getting caught in a lie is one of the most cited reasons for being honest.
- **Stop the executioner in their tracks** – Like the quote at the beginning of this chapter, if you own your mistakes right away you stop the momentum of those reading you the riot act. Wise employees know that this is one of the best things you can do to show maturity on the job.
- **Breeds trust** – When you have the trust of your staff, they don't spend as much time second guessing what you said. This leads to much quicker buy-in and quicker results.
- **You get a re-do** – Dishonest leaders don't get another chance to explain themselves when there is a misunderstanding, because logically they will just tell another lie. If you are an honest leader, you will get a chance to explain yourself again when there is a misunderstanding because it is logical for the team member to believe they will get more of the original truth.

It often seems easier to tell a "white lie" than to tell the whole truth, but as with most poor leadership techniques, it is short sighted. I hope this chapter gives you a few more arguments to stay on the course of honesty.

LESSON ASSIGNMENT: Can you come up with a place or situation where you are more prone to tell "white lies?" Are there more than one? Then go ahead and write these down. By keeping these places and situations on the top of your mind you'll be more prepared to stick to your guns and tell the truth instead of giving a "reflex white lie."

Do the Little Things Right

"Big jobs usually go to the men who prove their ability to outgrow small ones."
~Theodore Roosevelt

"Great acts are made up of small deeds." ~Lao Tzu

. . . . .

Why is your boss so obsessed with some of the little things? Well to put it succinctly:

- Because they are indicative of the bigger things.
- Because they add up.
- Because there is little excuse for not doing little things right.

Little things really aren't that little. If you think about your great employees, rarely is there one who was great at the big things, but was terrible at the routine tasks (it happens, but *very* infrequently). And it goes for leaders too. Great leaders are great all of the time. In your case, you set the bar from your staff's perspective, so if you aren't good at the little things neither will they, and they will probably be very unforgiving in their appraisal of you if you try to take them to task on their performance on the little things.

Your expertise when dealing with yourself and your staff should be in describing *why* the little things are important, or what *big* thing they set up for success. Three examples:

- If we don't file our paperwork correctly, then it'll take forever for us to find the Sales Order when there is a question about it.
- If we don't double check the items being received, then our inventory count may be off and we'll need to recount the entire warehouse.
- If we keep rounding the weight down, we are missing out on revenue.
    - I once heard that an airline saved $175,000 annually by reducing the number of olives on their in-flight salad by 1.

To put forward one last example of how to do it right: I recently saw a CNBC special on Wal-Mart and their operations, and one of the scenes involved a division manager talking to a room full of about 200 fabric department employees from different stores. As a demonstration of the importance of cutting off bulk fabric accurately, she had each of them hold up their thumb (apparently as you are measuring yards of fabric it isn't uncommon to give a couple of inches extra to speed the process along). The point was that if each of the 200 employees gave out a thumb's worth of extra fabric on the 5-10 fabric orders they processed a day, it added up to an awful lot of fabric.

So don't lose sight of the little things, as mentioned above, they really are the foundation for larger things.

LESSON ASSIGNMENT: Write down the top 10 "little things" in your department (maybe greeting, picking up the phone, double checking something) and see if you can create a method for ensuring your team has done it right.

OK, you don't get off that easy…..now make a list of your own top 10 "little things" and see if you can find a method for holding yourself accountable.

It Gets Harder Before It Gets Easier

"Difficulties increase the nearer we approach the goal." ~Goethe

"It is a bad plan that admits of no modification." ~Publilius Syrus

. . . . .

Constantly improving things is something we are called to do as leaders, but finding an area to improve on means that you will have to work and learn more than you are at this moment. Whenever you look to make improvements to people, products, and processes you almost always start the learning curve from the beginning, regardless of how well you prepare and train. Since you're at the beginning of the learning curve your team won't be as productive, your team won't be as quick, and your team will make more mistakes. Sometimes this leads the more disheartened leaders to be tempted to stop the progress and go back to the way things were before, this is often (but not always) a bad idea. Let's take a look at the three things I called out above.

- **Mistakes** – Probably the most frustrating aspect of improvement and change is the inevitable mistakes as new processes take hold. Oftentimes, what used to be the correct procedure is now incorrect. Document these instances to track improvement, but know that their frequency will decrease with time.
- **Slower** – Your staff will be second guessing themselves as their "muscle and mind memory" is getting accustomed to the new process. Again, if you can track the progress (and hopefully not lack thereof) you may be able to identify trouble areas that might

need some tweaking. Again, this will pass as your staff gets more familiar with the process.
- **Less Productive** – The effect of the above is that there may not be any immediate improvement to productivity, but realize that it may just be slow in coming.

Keep two things on your own mind and make sure your staff knows that they are on your mind:

- Where you are from a productivity standpoint while you are rolling this out may not be as good as where you *used to* be.
- But where you are right now is also not as good as where you *will* be once it has been rolled out all the way.

So what do you do when you find yourself lost in the uncomfortable "in-between" area? Do a little evaluating and modifying:

- Are there more or less problems than you thought there would be?
    - What does that say about where you are going?
    - Can any of them be easily fixed while the momentum is building?
- As issues come up, are you addressing them?
    - Training – Do you need more of it?
    - Modifications - To the procedure, product or plan? Is it easier to do that now? Maintaining flexibility is key.

The one thing you want to be careful of is to not pull the plug too soon, or become so negative about the problems occurring during roll-out that you end up shooting the process in the foot and either killing it, or lengthening out the time until it reaches peak efficiency. This isn't to say that you may not need to do an "about- face" on this endeavor, but you want to have the facts and give the new process time to catch on and bear fruit.

LESSON ASSIGNMENT: The next time you start an improvement in your organization, set your metric goals *below* where they are currently at and have a schedule for moving them up as you progress to account for the learning curve and everything that comes along with it.

Never as Bad as it Looks, and Never as Good Either

"Whenever an individual or a business decides that success has been attained, progress stops." ~Thomas J. Watson

"Ones best success comes after their greatest disappointments." ~ Henry Ward Beecher

. . . . .

Regardless of how your day, week, month, quarter or year is going, remember not only that things change, but that our view of the present is often fraught with inaccuracies. So when you find the elation of everything going your way, or the misfortune of everything falling apart, remember to "take a chill pill", "slow your roll" and otherwise relax. When you are at a new high or a new low, it is good to pause for perspective and evaluate where you are at as honestly as you can and look to the future so that you do not get stuck in the past, even if the past was a success.

When things are at their worst, pause and ask yourself:

- **What is going wrong?** Define the issue and look for causes. Maybe the problem doesn't lie where you thought it did originally. Either way, just defining what the problem is prevents you from thinking that *everything* is going wrong.
- **How can you fix it?** Coming up with a plan for dealing with the issue gets you focused on the solution and infuses *hope* into your thinking.
- **What is the end goal?** Define what you want the end result to look like. This ensures that your action plan is focused on the goal and gets your mind thinking in positive terms.
- **Look for opportunities** – Oftentimes there are opportunities and freedoms in the tough times that don't exist when things are going well. Look for the good in the bad.

When things are at their best, pause and ask yourself:

- **What is going right?** What things have led to this success? Has this success opened up new opportunities?
- **What *work* can you do to keep it going?** The most consistent leadership mistake across all industries is to rest on your laurels when things are good. You need to still put in the work to stay a success. The key is to look to keep doing what got you here and to strengthen it where you can.
- **What is your goal?** You may need to ensure the goal you're working towards is still valid. Or perhaps you have met your goal already, well great!!! Now it's time to get a new one!!! Without a goal out there, you have nothing to shoot for and are just adrift (and that is where success becomes a problem).

Bad times and good times don't last forever, *only* if actions ensure they don't. Make sure you are working toward your goal of continued success, or a turnaround from the decline you are in.

LESSON ASSIGNMENT: When things start going really well, or when things start going really bad, ask yourself what opportunities have just opened up? Also ask yourself what you have been doing that got you to this point. Maybe you need to do more of something or reverse course depending on where you are at.

Assume There is Always a Better Way

"There's no good idea that can't be improved on." ~Michael Eisner

"It is always safe to assume, not that the old way is wrong, but that there may be a better way." ~Henry F Harrower

. . . . .

You will seldom get in trouble for following the Standard Operating Procedures, but you will rarely get outstanding results. To truly excel you must look for a better way, constantly looking to improve the product and the process. Luckily it is safe to assume that there are indeed areas that can be improved upon.

Why assume it? Because *there is* always a better way! Whether it be time to completion, accuracy, or overall production, the complicated nature of today's business environment ensures that there are small and large tweaks to the system that can yield positive results. But how do you begin finding those areas where you have opportunities for improvement? Simple, you ask those around you. In order of importance:

- **Ask your staff** – The number one source for great ideas to improve operations are the people that are right in the thick of it all day.
  - **Ask in small groups, then individually** – One trick I have used in the past to great effect is to get people together in groups. I don't necessarily call it brainstorming, but a lot of times the ideas of one person will spark an idea in others. Then after these sessions I will follow up individually with everyone in case some people were shy or have come up with another idea.
- **Ask new employees after their first month** – A fresh pair of eyes is often best to uncover what we have stopped noticing throughout our days.
- **Ask your peers** – A neutral and outside point of view can be refreshing. Your peers also come from a perspective similar to yours, so they may be seeing things that front line employees are missing.
- **Ask yourself** – Seriously, take a step back and ask yourself where your "pain points" are in the operation (those things that constantly frustrate you) and ask how you can make them better.
- **Ask your boss** – Your boss will have a different perspective on the operation than you, your peers or your team have. So what they see and the ideas they have could be very unique and ones you wouldn't normally think of.

So after working through this exercise (you should have a laundry list after just meeting with your staff):

- **Now take action** – select an item and "Go". You can start with a simple item to start with a success or start with a highly impactful item, the key is to get going on this path and build it into the way you and your team work.
- **Don't overwhelm yourself (start with one at a time)** – You have an operation to run, so be careful that the running of the operation doesn't suffer while you make improvements. Oftentimes we need to take resources away from regular

operations to get improvements up and running. The key to this is to *define* how many resources and for how long you are going to have them working on the improvement. By doing this you control both areas and can ensure you don't short change either.

- **The key is to build momentum and habit** – Habits take time and one of the keys to getting across that time expanse is to keep momentum going, so plan for a mix of short wins and impactful wins and be sure to celebrate each and every accomplishment!

LESSON ASSIGNMENT: Meet with your team to brainstorm ideas. Then make one positive change each and every week. Then build to twice a week. I'd say move to three p/week, but in today's workplace reality there are tough days where you'll be lucky to keep your head above water with e-mail and emergencies, so it is best to keep it realistic. Go get'em!

Solutions are Useless if not Acted Upon

"Action is the foundational key to all success." ~ *Pablo Picasso*

"The really important things are said over cocktails and are never done." ~*Peter F. Drucker*

· · · · ·

Lots of us sit in meetings or at lunch and talk about "what to do", or "what we should do". But how often are these things put into place? If your organization is anything like mine, your percentage could stand to improve. So once we have a bunch of ideas, how do we improve the percentage of ideas that actually get put into place?

- **The quick and dirty way** is simply to assign it to someone - Too often a meeting is similar to the scene of an accident, where all 10 of you are there, but everyone thinks someone else has dialed 911 so it never gets called. If you have left a meeting where a solution was discussed, but not assigned, you have failed.
- **The more elaborate way** is to begin the plan – take the solution a step further and talk about a plan for implementing it. This covers the crucial "Well how do we actually *do* that" question and should end with everyone being clear what the next step is. Getting the ball rolling is always the toughest part and this helps with that. It also eliminates the first excuse, "I wasn't sure how to start" and gives a chance to split the workload a little depending on the size of the meeting to create more accountability.
- **The toughest way** is to let everyone's boss know the outcome - your boss is held accountable for results and wants to see you taking action, not just talking. This method keeps everyone on their toes and focused on putting something into place.

Most of us know what to do or at least have an idea of what to do, but too few of us actually go about implementing all of the solutions we come up with. As a leader you are paid to create positive results, the more solutions you put into place the more likely you are to get the results you want.

LESSON ASSIGNMENT: In the next meeting you attend or are leading, be sure that at the end of the agenda there is a line it labelled "Assigning Tasks." And make sure that no matter how much wasn't discussed there are at least a couple of minutes set aside for it.

The Right Steps Only Matter If You Get the Right Results

"However beautiful the strategy, you should occasionally look at the results." ~Winston Churchill

"Even if you're on the right track, you'll get run over if you just sit there." - Will Rogers

. . . . .

Only the naïve pay attention to talk as opposed to results. There are a decent percentage of leaders out there who know what the right thing is to do. Now in today's business world, that alone is good enough to separate you from many of your peers (sad as that fact is). What I see too much of though is that leaders get praised and rewarded so significantly for *doing* the right thing as opposed to getting the *result*, that they lose the motivation to move further. Now when I say "right" in this case I mean the correct action for the organization. This isn't getting into anything ethical. In fact, they see praise only halfway through their journey. The right thing is only the right thing if it leads to the desired result. While taking the correct action is good, it's the right result that we are really after. The focus shouldn't be on the right thing to do as an ending point, it should be on the actual end result. To misappropriate the focus is akin to giving only participation trophies instead of also giving 1st, 2nd and 3rd place trophies.

Some things to consider on this topic:

- **Define the outcome, not the action steps** – The important thing is the desired end result, not the next step. While those first steps are important, they only matter if you reach the goal. Define the end result you are looking for and work backwards, this ensures you are talking about the result first.
- **Deflect praise when it is too early** – It isn't being modest when you tell the boss that is praising you that you aren't done yet. This not only focuses you, but also your staff and those around you.
- **The right thing isn't always the right thing** - Business is littered with innovators who broke the rules, did things differently, and got fantastic results. If the correct action steps aren't getting the results, you have a duty to improvise.
- **A last illustration** - We all have employees who do what they are supposed to do, but *only* what they are supposed to do and nothing more. They focus on the process, not the results and are therefore only mediocre at best. Don't fall into the same trap as a leader, look to get results, and use the "right steps" as a guide to get there.

A results focused leader and department is a powerful entity that "gets things done." Don't lose your way on the journey by losing sight of what you are truly after, the result, not just doing the "right thing."

LESSON ASSIGNMENT: The right steps and right actions don't always work in the business world, but don't let that dissuade you. Hold yourself to a higher standard. The next time you are "pre-congratulated" tell them that they can congratulate you when you are finished. Do it politely, but try to do it publicly.

Anybody Can be a Skeptic, Leaders Create Solutions

"Great leaders are almost always great simplifiers who cut through argument, debate, and doubt to offer a solution everybody can understand." ~Unknown

"The value of a company is the sum of the problems you solve." ~Daniel Ek

. . . . .

If you are in an organization that rewards skeptics or people who spend their day poking holes in other people's ideas, then run as fast as you can to a competitor and put in a job application because to be blunt about it, your organization will be shrinking in size soon. Skeptics create no value, they only put a spotlight how quickly value is lost. Now while that *is* a part of what we should all be doing, the main focus should always be fostering on new ideas to solve organization problems or customer problems.

Now it is *very* easy to fall into the skeptical trap for several reasons:

- **Laziness** - It is always easier to tear something down than to build it up (and that definitely goes for new ideas as well). Poking holes in other people's ideas is the easiest way to get face-time or talk-time in meetings.
- **No investment** - It costs us nothing to be skeptical. By its very nature skepticism is only a half-hearted disagreement with the idea in question. If it works out, then the creator of the idea gets the credit, and the skeptic can be pleased and surprised at the success. If it doesn't work out, then the skeptic gets to be right.

- **Risk aversion** – People by nature are risk averse, and to spend time and resources on an idea is a risk. "Even the best laid plans go awry" as the old saying goes. So if you don't want to take that risk, just not doing anything is an easy way to address it.

But what every good organization needs, and the better ones crave, are new ideas that create value. So while we could talk about brainstorming new ideas, what I would like to talk about is a couple of techniques to turn that natural pull of skepticism into a more positive leadership of new ideas:

- **Solutions not just problems** – It is fine to point out an issue that exists with another person's plan, but *offer a solution* or offer to help find one. Don't just shoot down without building up.
- **Seek ownership** – Going along with the above point, if you find a problem take ownership of finding its solution.
- **Tell people what you are doing** – Oftentimes it is safest to not talk about the simple projects you have going on as it opens you up to criticism, but if you do, you exercise the visibility and risk muscles in your brain and it helps you to step out the next time you have an idea in the meeting.
- **Focus on positive effort** – Work is easier when we are making a positive contribution. Fixing a problem is always a constructive thing.

Leaders create solutions to problems both inside and outside the organization, they create value. That is where your experience and knowledge find their most valuable use. Do not short-change yourself and the organization by taking the easy way out by just being skeptical of other people's ideas.

LESSON ASSIGNMENT: Institute a rule that you cannot find fault with an idea unless you propose its solution or an alternate idea. Mediate this in discussions you overhear and demonstrate this in your own behavior.

Have No Enemies

"We build too many walls and not enough bridges." ~Sir Isaac Newton

"If everyone is moving forward together, then success takes care of itself." ~Henry Ford

. . . . .

Of course your competitor is your "enemy", but there is no need for other enemies inside the organization. Now I draw a difference between not liking someone, and having an enemy. You won't get along with everyone you work with, but working with those people you don't necessarily get along with is one of the things that define leadership. People err in their business when they let things fester for too long and begin to think of their teammates as their foes.

The issues with having enemies:

- **They take away energy and concentration from the business** – Perhaps the most impactful issue with enemies is the effort it takes to fight them. Now some may say, "It's no big deal Cameron, that sort of competition is what elevates everyone's game". To that I say that *competition* is absolutely helpful when it is constructive, but the passion that comes along with a "fight" is rarely constructive.
- **They have a negative effect on morale** – If you and your enemy are constantly bashing each other around the office, you are focusing on negativity around your team. "What does he say about us when we are not around" may be one of the things they

are saying. The other may be "Aren't we supposed to be on the same team?" In either case, constructive improvement of the organization is *not* what is being focused on by those around you, and that should *always* be the focus.
- **They hurt you politically** – The employee that has enemies is often considered to have "made" enemies whether they have or haven't, and few organizations consider that a good trait in a leader. Also, an enemy often actively works against you behind the scenes, undermining your authority and success.

Positives of not having enemies:

- **Proves to everyone that you can build bridges** – There is a reason that teamwork has become a cornerstone in Business Schools, because it works. Those that can build teams are the ones who get tapped for promotions. Think of the boss who is looking around for someone to promote and realizes "I can't find anyone who doesn't like this guy", now that's a good problem for you.
- **Eliminates distraction** – The opposite of the energy and concentration issue above. You can stay focused on the most beneficial use of your time for the organization.
- **Sets the right example for your team** – They are always watching you for clues on how they should behave and react around their peers. Set an example that will keep them focused on using their best abilities for the good of the organization.

Some leaders feed off of the adrenaline of taking competition too far and create enemies all around them. These leaders rarely meet with long term success because they demonstrate that they don't have the people skills to lead larger teams within the organization. Also, they spend so much energy on their "fight" that they don't have any energy left to create exceptional results. Build bridges with those who could be your enemy, you'll go much further.

Step Up Before Your Employees Step Down

LESSON ASSIGNMENT: Make a list of anyone who might consider you an enemy or who you might have "rubbed the wrong way" for whatever reason. This might be easy or it might be difficult, but the key is to mend fences as soon as possible. Look to do this exercise at the beginning of every month so that no ill feelings are allowed to take root.

The Manager's Diary II

The Staff

Managing For Success

The Manager's Diary II

Don't Even Think About Reading This

"Reason and judgment are the qualities of a leader." ~Tacitus

"Strong reasons make strong actions." ~Shakespeare

. . . . .

So why are you reading this? The message was clear that you shouldn't be reading this right now? So why did you continue reading?

I never gave you a "reason" for my warning that you could understand and accept.

We do this a lot as leaders. We make a decision or set a policy without giving the "reason" for it to our team. Then curiosity or lack of conviction causes our team to go against the directive, often with detrimental impact on the organization. While they are obligated to follow our directions based on positional power, without strong convictions they oftentimes slip into old habits, or even worse, simply ignore the directive.

How many of us have received a task or directive from our boss and thought that it was stupid? Most of us I would guess. Now in most of those incidences, were you given the reason for the task or directive? My guess is that most of the time you weren't. And for those times you were, I'd bet the reason was shallow and incomplete. The extra 30-60 seconds it takes to explain the reason fully pays off in a lot of extra saved time.

Once you start a habit of giving the reasons behind your actions, you will find that you get better compliance and build trust amongst your staff. While compliance is the immediate goal, it is in the building of trust that you reap long term benefits.

If you want people to follow your instructions, explain why you are giving the instructions. It's as simple as that.

LESSON ASSIGNMENT: Today (if it is the weekend, do this with your children) when you ask someone to do something, tell them why you are asking specifically for them to do it and why it is important. Do this all day long to get some momentum with this moving forward.

Be a Voyeur Manager

"When people talk, listen completely. Most people never listen." ~Ernest Hemingway

"Either you deal with what is the reality or you can be sure that the reality is going to deal with you." ~Alex Haley

. . . . .

The flip side of finding the time to be alone and think is being present and observant within your own department and putting your finger on the pulse of what is occurring there. A great leader knows the larger context of his/her actions and adjusts subtly or dramatically according to what they see on the "field of play". The work gets assigned and the issue gets addressed, but the approach may change depending on what is going on in the department.

We do this on a person by person basis all of the time; changing our approach depending on the person's personality to get our point across best. Taking it to the next level by changing approach at a department level is the natural next step. But how do you get your finger on the pulse of your department? I recommend three techniques that have worked for me:

- **Pause at points in your day to listen** – I have set a reminder to pause every 1.5 hours and just listen, maybe just for 30 seconds. It keeps you in touch with what is going on by gauging tone of voice, the amount of chatter, volume, etc. Sometimes when it is loud and chatty it is good (energy, productivity and passion), sometimes bad (arguing, getting upset, distracting themselves from work). Sometimes silence is golden (they are all focused on their work) or it is bad (they lack energy or are defeated). The only way to separate the two is to listen regularly.
- **Look at body language** – Does your staff look energized? Exhausted? Confused? Angry? Body language is often the lie detector for all of your other observations. They may be able to say the right words, but their body may tell a different story.
- **Look at activity** – Is it frenetic like an anthill that has been kicked? Is it sedentary like a funeral home? Similar to the example regarding loudness and silence above, both can be good or bad, the key is to notice and change accordingly.

It's easy for us to get so caught up in our day to day activities that we forget to look around, and even when we do we may not be consciously getting information from it. The simple act of looking and listening to your team can help you get ahead of so many problems and become an even more effective leader with little to no downside.

Once you see or hear what is going on, you must then take action to address what you see and hear. You'll find as you do it more and more it becomes increasingly natural. So give it a try, you'll see what I'm talking about.

LESSON ASSIGNMENT: Set a reminder for the morning and the afternoon to walk through your department and say "Hi" to a few team members, but really *look and listen* at what is going on in your area of responsibility.

Over-Communicate or You Risk Not Communicating Enough

"The simple act of paying positive attention to people has a great deal to do with productivity" ~Tom Peters

"Good leaders make people feel that they're at the very heart of things, not at the periphery." ~Warren Bennis

. . . . .

While I don't want to say that there is absolutely no way you can over-communicate, but 99% of the time that's the case. If you don't feel like you are over-communicating, you aren't communicating *remotely* enough. If there is any doubt, communicate some more, what is the worst that could happen?

When you exercise the maximum amount of communication, your staff knows:

- **What is going on** – You eliminate uncertainty, reduce rumors, and bring them into the discussion. Ignorance of what is going on is one of the chief complaints of employees under bad management.
- **What you're thinking** – They don't need to worry about what you think of them, what your vision for the department/company is, and most importantly, they begin to understand *how* you think which allows them to look ahead and anticipate.
- **Where Opportunities/Dangers Lie** – You can convey areas where mistakes could occur and where you think the greatest opportunities for success are.
- **Where they can help** – When they know what is going on, and they know what your vision is, they can start seeing where their skills can be used and they can start offering solutions of their own.

Communication is a two way street though, so listen just as much or more than you talk. Ask questions, give updates, and solicit ideas. A team that communicates more than another is going to have a distinct advantage over their competition. So I'll stop right here so you can go out and talk to your team. Get to it, it's one of the simplest ways to improve the production of your team.

LESSON ASSIGNMENT: Pick two of the categories above where you think you may be able to improve the most. Now come up with two actions you can take against each of these this week to begin seeing improvement?

Why Fun is Important to any Team

"There is little success where there is little laughter." ~Andrew Carnegie

"The ability to summon positive emotions during periods of intense stress lies at the heart of effective leadership." ~Jim Loehr

. . . . .

People spend most of their waking life at work and if they aren't fulfilled and enjoying themselves, then they simply aren't as productive as possible. In that respect instilling a sense of fun at work makes good business sense. So what exactly are the benefits?

- **Fun builds teamwork** – Shared laughter and games build a strong community. It is this community building that reaps benefits when the going gets tougher and your staff readily needs to rely more on one another.
- **Fun breaks up the monotony** – Everyone likes variety, and it serves the business purpose of keeping the mind flexible and engaged. If your people are constantly stuck in a rut, they will not be able to see opportunities and change when the business needs change.
- **Fun exposes new aspects of individuals** – You'd be surprised, no I'll say *shocked*, at what strengths and talents your staff possesses that you are unaware of. Oftentimes it is only when the walls of formality come down that these get exposed. If you want to know what potential exists in your people, you need to get them out of the monotony of their work.

OK, so I have you sold on the concept (shouldn't have been too tough, who doesn't like to have fun?), now what should be the framework of your "fun program"?

- **Do *at least* one fun thing a month** - Movie night, dress up day, video game competition, trivia contest, go-cart racing, bowling, something. It needs to be a regular thing so that you are constantly refueling everyone's tanks.
- **Something where people form teams or have a common experience that ties them together** – Teamwork should be one of the focuses of the exercises as that is one of the principle benefits of the "fun program" you are starting. It doesn't absolutely need to be team related, but there needs to be a shared experience at bare minimum.
- **Do it at work and/or on work time** – The reason I add this in is for two reasons: 1) that it ensures participation from everyone and 2) that it ensures that the "fun" is associated with the staff's work environment and focuses on the fact that *work* is fun and energetic.
- **Get some good P.R. out there ahead of time** – You never get a second chance to make a great first impression, so you need to let everyone know about it, build excitement, buy-in, and participation. *You* and your leadership will set the tone for the event. The first time you try this is the most important, so really sell out.

Again, having some fun at work makes great business sense. A good community of employees supports one another, has lower attrition, and is more engaged. Now *that's* good leadership.

LESSON ASSIGNMENT: Come up with a "Fun Calendar" that you can keep in your office. This visually helps you keep a steady stream of fun going in your organization. Schedule things in advance, publicize them ahead of time, ask for volunteers, ask for suggestions, etc.

Find the Engine of Action

"If your actions inspire others to dream more, learn more, do more and become more, you are a leader." ~John Quincy Adams

"You must have long range goals to keep you from being frustrated by short range failures." ~Charles C. Noble

• • • • •

What turns your crank and gets the juices flowing? What is it for the team? What inspires them to give their all? Is it doughnuts? Is it beating international sales targets? Crushing the competition? Finding this and leveraging it is the rocket fuel for exceptional results. This isn't necessarily just a productivity thing. It makes problems less draining, it makes tedious tasks "seem" to go faster, and it breeds positivity.

Why is that? It provides a goal and something to reach for to keep your mind engaged on the positive end result, not any negativity going on in the present. The more personally exciting the goal, the better. So what should the process be for finding and putting into use the "crank turning" initiative?

- **Try something out, then try another** – I started this chapter off with a few possible suggestions, but one of the important things I learned is that "good is the enemy of better" and it doesn't hurt to continue to experiment, even when you have found a successful avenue. Never stop experimenting. The worst that can happen is that variety keeps things fresh.

- **Does it get results?** – Many leaders try something "fun" and it *is fun*, but we're looking for results. Always lay out a plan for what you expect ahead of time, and if you don't end up meeting your expectations, make any necessary tweaks or changes.
- **Does it get chatter?** – Look for results you didn't expect, sometimes the benefit is in what may have seemed to be an unrelated area. One of the best ways to find these is to "listen to the chatter." Results usually elicit excitement, which results in the team talking about it.
- **Do a couple of things, mix it up** – Don't be afraid to try a two-in-one technique where you use a couple of ideas simultaneously, just be careful of watering it down. You are looking for complimentary activities like upsells and sales for example.
- **Break it apart and make it better** – Every great idea, process, and product can be made better. Once you have an idea that works, make it more public, add metrics to it, report hourly, etc. You want to get maximum leverage out of it.

Find your staff's "engine of action" and you'll find a way to not just get better results, but have a happier team to boot. Realize also that it is likely to vary quite a bit amongst different members of your team so be ready to vary your approach regularly to not only keep it fresh, but to touch each member of your team.

LESSON ASSIGNMENT: Ask your team what trackable metric they pay the most attention to? This is their business related interest. Now what can you do surrounding this to get them even more excited about it? Come up with three contest ideas surrounding the most popular of these things and have the team vote on which contest they want to run over the next 30 days. You can have this up and running this week, so get to it.

You are the Shock Absorber

"Leadership is a matter of having people look at you and gain confidence in how you react. If you're in control, they're in control." ~Tom Landry

"If you don't understand that you work for your mislabeled "subordinates", then you know nothing of leadership. You know only tyranny." ~Dee Hock

. . . . .

One of the hallmarks of a great leader is that you are able to get the absolute best out of your team. Training is essential, procedures are vital, and feedback is a must. But what separates great leaders from the pretenders is how much they manage the environment so that their team can use what they have learned to their maximum ability.

In most cases this means shielding your team from stressors large and small. We have all had that boss that created *more* stress and an environment where we could not work at maximum effectiveness. Great leaders accomplish the opposite by being the "shock absorber" for their staff and smoothing out the jarring effects of day to day business. The three most common areas where they do so:

- **Simplify the chaotic** – When things really get humming in an organization, the pace of activity can create chaos if there isn't someone there to give specific direction and prioritize. Finding a way to focus your staff on specific items cuts out duplicate work and indecision. Clarity is what you should be seeking to give.

- **Take the risk on yourself** – Ultimately the ownership over your team's output is yours. If your staff is constantly worried about making a mistake or derailing an important project, they will spend half their time second guessing themselves and working in fear. *Not* optimal environments for productivity. Use oversight and check-in (don't micromanage) and own the success or failure of your team. Remember, in sports it is the coach who gets fired when the team loses.
- **De-stress the stressful** – Looming deadlines and pressure for perfection should be yours to worry about. Stress can bring out the best sometimes, but too much of it causes cracks to form. A staff that is rushing to meet a deadline often makes mistakes or puts out substandard work. Similarly, perfection can be either inspiring or paralyzing. Manage for just the right stress by using the oversight above and leaving out the superfluous stuff that just makes everybody sweat.

Be the shock absorber for your staff so that they can fly down the rough road of business and not get tossed all around the inside of the car.

LESSON ASSIGNMENT: One area we are all constantly under pressure from are looming deadlines. In an effort to be the shock absorber for your team, the next time a deadline is approaching and you feel the stress level of the team increasing, lay out the plan to completion in a step by step fashion. If they see you are calm and they see the plan laid out in front of them, their stress level should diminish.

Keep People Engaged and Excited

"As a leader, you're probably not doing a good job unless your employees can do a good impression of you when you're not around." ~Patrick Lencioni

"Tell me and I forget. Teach me and I remember. Involve me and I learn." - Benjamin Franklin

. . . . .

Any leader worth their salt has an engaged workforce. I define an "engaged" worker as someone who is never going through the motions, they are aware of how the organization is doing, how the department is doing, and how they are doing. They know what products sell well and which don't, they individualize the customer experience, and above all, they provide feedback to their fellow employees and their boss. So how do you get one of these magical employees you ask? Well you work *long* and *hard* at it, that's how. Engagement isn't a one way street, it takes as much effort on your part as anyone else's:

- **Performance updates** – The organization, the division, the department, and the employee. They need to receive information on what is going well and what isn't to be able to act upon it.
- **Flexible procedures** – Scripting the interactions between your employees and your customers is the best way to tell them you want them to be robots….and robots aren't the engaged workforce that will help you excel. Give guidelines, give points that you want them to hit with each interaction, but show them that you trust them to craft the interaction in their own way.

Your control over this flexibility comes from the regular performance updates above.

- **Ask for their feedback** – Ask in team meetings, ask in individual meetings, ask whenever you can how they think you could do things better, what is working and what isn't.
- *Then act on the feedback* – Once people see that someone else's idea was put into place, they will be far more likely to offer their own suggested improvements. Don't forget to give the original person *all* of the credit (reward what you want to see more of).
- **Just talk to them about whatever** – And don't forget the human element of just showing that you are interested in what is going on in their lives. Establishing a relationship with your staff encourages engagement.

Employee engagement reduces turnover, speeds training, improves selling techniques, reduces errors, and gets us closer to World Peace (OK, that may be taking it a step too far). But it is truly one of the best things you can foster within your department to improve performance....so start engaging!

LESSON ASSIGNMENT: Regimented procedures are necessary in many places, but they can stifle innovation. Instead of making firm procedures which must be dogmatically adhered to, try giving them the desired result in as great a detail as possible and "suggest" procedures that can get them to the goal. This gives them more freedom which can lead to more engagement and satisfaction.

Tackle Unnecessary Obstacles

"One of the most important tasks of a manager is to eliminate his people's excuses for failure." ~Robert Townsend

"A leader is not an administrator who loves to run others, but one who carries water for his people so that they can get on with their jobs" ~Anonymous

• • • • •

Your team can climb the mountain, but sometimes the underbrush is so impenetrably thick that you can't set about getting to the top. Just as those little vines when multiplied, impede your progress, so too do the little nuisances on the job undermine your ability to achieve greatness. In our efforts as leaders to make the next great leap forward, we often forget to look for opportunities where we can simply take a small step or two forward and end up in the same place.

Some places to look for those vines that are holding your team back: privilege

- **Revisiting empowerment** – Do there need to be some supervisor/management approved exceptions to rules? Would the team benefit from just a slight amount of increased flexibility or empowerment? Controls are important, but can become restrictive if left unchecked.
- **Simple cost effective tools** – Hey I'm not talking about buying a new $5,000 printer so that their print jobs can finish faster, sometimes post-it notes and calculators work. Are there simple tools that your people are clamoring for? Honestly,

they have usually asked for them so many times, and think they are so small, that it may take them some new thinking to come up with them. So ask them.
- **Dogmatic procedures** – Generally, the fewer steps in the process the better. Are there any unnecessary steps you make your staff go through to get their work done? If you haven't looked at it in the last 6 months I bet there is.

Great leaps forward are fun, but they are also a lot of work and take time and planning. Sometimes you can accomplish just as much by making a minor change or adding a small tool. As a great manager, you should look for both the leap and the small step.

LESSON ASSIGNMENT: Just like the vine example above, there are a multitude of obstacles that are in front of your team constantly. Ask each of them this week what they think are "unnecessary obstacles" that they deal with regularly. Some of these you may not be able to address, but if you reach out to every team member, I bet there will be a few.

Believe in the Unbelievable

"First they ignore you, then they laugh at you, then they fight you, then you win."
~Mahatma Gandhi

"You don't lead by pointing and telling people some place to go. You lead by going to that place and making a case." ~Ken Kesey

We all have a natural fear of embarrassment, pain, and the unknown. I mention this because this tendency makes us resistant to change and new ideas. Creating plans towards processes and products that do not currently exist is what can make quantum leaps forward for your organization/department. You need to be the one to push the envelope of progress.

Your belief and conveyance of your belief to your team is the *single most important factor* in unbelievable ideas becoming a reality. Great leaders believe in the unbelievable. They are first to see what is possible and to lay out the path to getting there. Their conviction fuels the efforts of those around them until success is realized or lessons are learned. But how do we exercise our belief in the unbelievable? How do we find the path that leads there? I recommend the following exercises to break through that initial disbelief:

- **What if you had unlimited people, money, and resources?** Taking away limitations is one of the keys to brainstorming. Too often we use the constraints of "reality" to limit our thinking. Once you come up with an idea you can see how to reduce or eliminate the constraints from there.
- **What could be better in a perfect world?** Other times the constraints are procedurally related. If everything functioned perfectly, could it be done? Then build a plan to shore up areas that break it down, or come up with workarounds.
- **Have you revisited the ideas that didn't work in the past?** There are lessons to be learned there, or there may be an opportunity for the time to be right this time.
- **Do you have past successes that you can use as an example?** How did you plot the course to the "unbelievable" before? Use this as a guide and as motivation to the staff for those naysayers who say it can't be done.

Most advances have seemed impossible before they came to fruition. Believe in your staff's ability to achieve great things and they will be far more likely to meet and exceed those expectations.

LESSON ASSIGNMENT: What are three big initiatives that were tried in the past, but ultimately failed? Pick one of these that seems the most likely to be a success in the current environment and take it through the process above and get to work making the unbelievable believable.

Feed Random Employee Passions

"One person with passion is better than forty people merely interested." ~E. M. Forster

"Let a man lose everything else in the world but his enthusiasm and he will come through again to success." ~H. W. Arnold

. . . . .

One of the best employee development tricks is to feed any passion they may have no matter how big, small, or strange and out of place it may be. Passion fuels exceptional performance plain and simple, and even if it isn't a part of the most impactful business areas it is essential that you capitalize on it. Why? Because passion is infectious both to the person experiencing it and those around him/her. It's hard to be down and uninspired when the person next to you is enjoying the heck out of their work at that moment. How do you feed it? By being supportive and by jumping at the opportunity to help the employee develop the passion, or at least spend more time in their passionate activity. It is elusive, random and far too rare in this day and age, but it is there if you keep an eye out for it and be ready when it appears. So how do you find it? Ask these questions to start:

- **Does someone love a particular product?** Have them be the "lead" and train others. Have them spend more time selling or working on that product. What will you get? A product evangelist.
- **Does someone excel at a particular task?** If they are doing it really well, it is often an indication of enjoyment of it. Give them an open ended option to do more of it if they like. Maybe instead of one day a week, they can do two or three. Maybe they can take it over for a couple of their peers.
- **Does someone excel at a service?** Sometimes people just love manning the tech support line, being the store greeter, even stocking the shelves (for the OCD among us) or even fixing the office printer. Offer more time in these areas.

The key is to not make them specialists necessarily, but to allow them to spend a little more time in those areas they are passionate about, and to leverage that time to elevate the department's performance. Energy is contagious, and if we encourage more energy and passion we will all become "infected."

LESSON ASSIGNMENT: Send out a survey this week asking for each team member's three favorite duties and their three least favorite duties. It's important they know that there is no judgement. What you hope to do is to find matches where you can increase someone's exposure to a task they like by 50% and minimize someone else's exposure that doesn't like that same task by 50%. You want passionate performance of every duty, but don't want to eliminate it completely since you still want to encourage your team to be well rounded.

Leverage Strengths and Weaknesses

"To succeed in life we must stay within our strength zone but move out of our comfort zone." ~John Maxwell

"The secret of success in life is for a man to be ready for his opportunity when it comes." ~Benjamin Disraeli

. . . . .

Do you know what your team's strength is? Do you know their weakness? If you are like most leaders, you probably have an idea, but have never formally thought about it or written it down. This is essential to the proper management of your area. Other than understanding your area, there are some *very* practical applications to clarifying strengths and weaknesses that can help you make quick and accurate decisions.

- **You know what new responsibilities you can take on** – Business is constantly changing to its environment which presents opportunities for those willing to seize them. When another department needs assistance, you'll know where you can lend a hand (hint: *don't* do it out of an area you are weak in). When a brand new business opportunity comes along, you'll know whether your department has a likelihood of being successful.
- **Kill a weakness with a strength** – Sometimes your strengths and weaknesses can be matched up and made complimentary to neutralize the weakness. For instance: having a large staff can be matched up to address a number of weakness by simply killing it with numbers, need more reporting, task some

staff, need to trim payroll, reduce hours slightly across the board, etc.
- **Create a strength from a weakness** – The opposite of that would be to create a strength out of a perceived weakness. A small staff can be more flexible than a large staff, can roll out new initiatives quicker, and can be held more accountable.
- **Do more of what you're good at** – The idea is to spend as much time as possible with your strengths and find ways to take on more strength centric activities. Overall it will make the whole organization better.

We already do a lot of this subconsciously, but if we start making the conscious effort to address it we can be even more intentional and impactful with it.

LESSON ASSIGNMENT: Write a list, come up with three strengths and three weaknesses for your organization, it may take five minutes, it may take five days. It clarifies what opportunities you should jump on and how to best tackle anticipated and unanticipated difficulties.

Manage Your Good News Delivery

"For a manager to be perceived as a positive manager, they need a four to one positive to negative contact ratio." ~Ken Blanchard

"No matter how thirsty you are, it is best to drink from the fountain as opposed to the fire hose" ~Cameron Morrissey

Step Up Before Your Employees Step Down

· · · · ·

I have spoken before about laying out all of the bad news at one time and *not spreading it out*. The flip side of that is that it is often best to spread out the good news over a period of time so as to create a positive pattern for your staff. Now I am not in favor of withholding good news, but in the course of project planning or task planning it is often possible and best to plan for it to be spread out to get maximum impact.

This came to my mind when speaking with a friend of mine who works in Silicon Valley. Her company had rolled out some positive benefits news a couple of months ago, and just last week announced they were rolling out a stock repurchase program next month, and she had heard from her friend in HR that in the 3rd quarter they were announcing that they were adding vacation time. Do you think their employees dread when announcements come out? (and yes, like you, I'd love to work for that company too)

They could have announced what they were working on for the whole year when they rolled out the first bit of news, but then they wouldn't have any good news for an entire year. Instead, they chose to announce as they finished each project, which means a steady stream of *very* good news which creates a positive environment for their staff. To draw an analogy: Giving all of the good news at once would be like giving the staff a sugar high with the inevitable crash right after.

Now this may seem somewhat contrived, but it's also smart. Great leaders manage as many things as possible to achieve the maximum effectiveness of their team. For those of us in more line-level management positions we can accomplish the same thing. We have a pretty good idea what initiatives, projects, policies and tasks will be viewed positively or negatively by our team. While we want to handle what's most important first, also throw some consideration on the positive and negative aspects of it on your staff and make small adjustments to timing accordingly. When it comes to good news in managing your staff, a steady stream beats a flood.

LESSON ASSIGNMENT: The next time you see some good news coming your way, try to set it up so that it falls on multiple days instead of just one. This can often be accomplished most easily by giving some of the good news out at the end of the day, then following up with the rest on the following morning. Even a small distinction like that creates a pattern.

Jump Under the Bus

"A good manager is a man who isn't worried about his own career but rather the careers of those who work for him." ~H.S.M. Burns

"A real leader faces the music, even when he doesn't like the tune." ~Author Unknown

. . . . .

Great leaders, and I mean *great* leaders, not only never throw anyone under the bus, but actively throw themselves under the bus in place of their staff. Do you know any leader like this? Would you admire them if you saw them? The fact that it is so rare is a testament to how difficult it really is.

So why do they do this? *Ownership & Example*

- **Any mistake in their area of oversight is their fault** - They should have seen it coming, should have prepared better, should have audited work better, or should have set up better processes. They understand that there is always something they could have done to prevent the mistake from occurring, and while the employee or peer may have had culpability as well, ultimately they are the leader and they are ultimately responsible.
- **Setting an example of accountability for their staff to follow** – If your boss is owning *any* mistake that could possibly be their fault, how much easier is it for you to see that owning up to mistakes is OK. Just as you take a wide area of responsibility, your team will begin to emulate that and take accountability for overall department performance not just their area.
- **Letting the staff know that they are supported** – You are demonstrating that they do not stand alone. This can be incredibly freeing for your staff, mitigates fear of failure, encourages ownership and based on both of these facets, significantly increases productivity.
- **Building Goodwill** – How much harder would you work for someone who took the heat for you? Or at bare minimum stood alongside you? Just saying.

This isn't easy, especially in a corporate environment that uses a heavy hand regarding mistakes, but the maturity you show by doing so can reap enormous benefits for the productivity of your department and your career. To use a battle analogy: Your staff is not cannon fodder, lead them from the front lines. Just as their success is your success, their failure will be yours as well.

LESSON ASSIGNMENT: The key here is taking ownership of what goes on around you. The first step is to take ultimate responsibility for what your team produces, good and bad. Get some practice taking ownership of any mistakes. You'll quickly find that when you do you have extra motivation to solve the root cause sooner and this will lead to big improvements down the road.

Make all of the Negative Changes at Once

"Bad news isn't wine. It doesn't improve with age." ~Colin Powell

"Always do right. This will gratify some people and astonish the rest." ~Mark Twain

. . . .

Eventually in your career you will be tasked with doling out some bad news. Now most of the time it is just a "one off" thing that comes up, but sometimes it is far more pervasive than that; new management, strategy change, budget cuts, etc. Since no one likes to give bad news, there is a temptation to only give out the news you absolutely have to at that moment, and save the rest of the bad news till later. To cut to the chase: Don't.

When your staff gets over bad news just to receive a new round of it, then gets over the new bad news just to get even more, you're setting up a situation where your staff is in a state of constant fear while they wait for the next "shoe to drop". When you have bad news, it is best to get it out of the way all at once (gets a load off of your shoulders as well). You're not doing your staff any favors by "managing the flow" of bad news.

With that said, I have a few tips on how to best handle the disseminating of bad news:

- **Let them know *why*** – The first thing to do is to let them know why this is happening, and be as honest as possible. Your staff is going to talk and come up with crazy rumors if you don't (and probably will do so even if you tell them), but most importantly it gives them the assurance that there was a "thought out" reasoning behind the change. They may not agree with it, but at least they know it was there and wasn't just done for no reason at all.
- **Let them know the *plan*** – Then let them know what to look for in the future. Let them know that there is a plan and what it is. Again, they may not agree with it, but at least they will know. This takes away the concern about "the other shoe dropping" and lets them know someone is still steering the ship.
- **Show them the end *goal*** – Paint the picture for them of how things will be once complete and all the way through the process. Try to put a little positive spin on it, but not so much as to be lying. This lets them know that there is something to shoot for, look forward to, etc. in the future.

Bad news isn't uncommon, and many employees won't be surprised by it (the paranoid and observant may be relieved it wasn't worse). The main thing is to take away as many of the unknowns as possible. Those unknowns are usually the scariest and most disruptive things for your staff. Then you are free to get on with the business of doing business.

LESSON ASSIGNMENT: Start with some "little" bad news events to get you some practice before tackling the "larger" bad news events. Once you have an issue that you need to address with the team, go through the "why", "plan" and "goal" steps.

Failure is Not an Option

"One of the most important tasks of a manager is to eliminate his people's excuses for failure." ~Robert Townsend

"Men meet with failure because of their lack of persistence in creating new plans to take the place of those which fail." ~Napolean Hill

. . . . .

One of the most powerful liberators of creativity and productivity is when failure is simply not an option. While failure is not something to be ashamed of (those who risk boldly often fail miserably) when you learn and grow from it, it is also not something to fall back on. So many department cultures have a "ho-hum" mentality towards performance. They work at it, they think about it, but they don't commit to it in the "we can't fail" ethos. What this does is, of course, leave performance improvements unrealized, but it also:

- **Stifles creativity and innovation** – When you have no choice but to succeed, you are forced to come up with innovative ways to ensure that you reach the finish line.
- **Limits feelings of success** – Little risks, little successes, big risks, big successes. If you aren't setting bold goals, you're selling your successes short.
- **Limits teamwork and collaboration** – A "No Fail" attitude forces your staff to reach out when they usually wouldn't. It also sets up a common set of experiences, in effect, it becomes a teambuilding exercise, just not on a rope course or bowling outing.

- **Eliminates a sense of urgency** – If you accept failure, you lose the sense of urgency of reaching for success. Think about how much you can do when you are under a deadline. Foster this in your staff and you've really increased performance.
- **Doesn't improve problem solving skills** – As the quote above says, failure is usually the result of not reacting to problems when they come up.

Oftentimes the difference between a successful leader and an unsuccessful one is their *tolerance* for failing, not the failure itself. When failure is not an option people can move mountains, completely redesign processes, and feel more excited and energized about their work than ever before. So how do you do it? Threats *are not* an option that reaps long term rewards. What I recommend is:

- **Tell them it isn't going away** – Too many times, our initiatives are the "flavor of the month" and your staff doesn't commit because they know this. Ensure they know that it is going to last.
- **Show them their progress and failure daily** – You must give them feedback, this reinforces the behavior you want, and discourages the behavior you don't.
- **Continuously reinforce the "Why"** – If they know why it is so important, they will buy in and understand why failure is not an option.
- **Bring them into the solution process (and show them how you do it)** – Tap their creativity and resolve, look to them for feedback on what is working. A "No fail" attitude makes you all a part of the team.

While the "no fail" attitude can seem a little extreme for most business settings, I believe it is better to have that attitude than one that tolerates failure as something that is normal, and I believe you should too.

LESSON ASSIGNMENT: List out all of the initiatives that were started over the last three months. Which ones failed? Pick one that you can restart and chart progress on it daily utilizing the principles above.

Lay the Foundation for Success

"Don't judge each day by the harvest you reap but by the seeds that you plant." - Robert Louis Stevenson

"Success is the sum of small efforts, repeated day in and day out." ~Robert Collier

. . . . .

The other day I was just a little "off". I didn't have the usual energy and focus that I usually do to drive day in day out results. But what do you think happened to the operation while I was in my "funk"? We had one of our most productive days ever! These results were brought about by the groundwork I had laid on the days, weeks, and months prior. So like a car going downhill, I took my foot off the gas, and the car just kept gaining speed.

Now I'm not recommending that you randomly decide to take days off, but when you focus on consistent excellence and continuous improvement you build a culture of success, so that even when you aren't in the operation, your people carry on the momentum. The basic building blocks for your staff are:

- **Do they know what to do?** They need to know what the priorities are and the necessary task lists.

- **Do they know how to do it?** They need to have been given the training, policies, and procedures to take care of business without your assistance or the assistance of their peers.
- **Do they have the tools to do it?** They need to be given the systems, reports, physical tools, and inventory to do their job exceptionally well.
- **Do they get feedback on their performance?** They need to know that you are watching and they need to know how well they are doing (knowing what success looks like).
- **Are they looking for improvements?** You must encourage them to improve processes, institute their suggestions, and give them credit for it.

If you manage to do all of these things, you will soon begin reaping *far* more than you sow and your productivity as a team will be constantly ramping up. So even when days don't go as planned, you will have put in the preparation necessary to still get great results.

LESSON ASSIGNMENT: Start with the first item on the list. Not having the right priorities or not being told what to do in a given situation allows for productivity slippage as people both try to figure out what to do and guess wrong. Getting this first step down cures the biggest problems and gives your team its biggest push forward. If you have already clearly established priorities, then please tackle the item that jumped out most on the list.

Own the Stories

"One of the best ways to persuade others is with your ears-by listening to them." ~ Dean Rusk

"Be careful the environment you choose for it will shape you. Be careful the friends you choose for you will become like them." ~W. Clement Stone

· · · · ·

When was the last time you shared a positive story with your team? If you haven't, then you aren't controlling the narrative within your department. They are telling each other stories all the time. Usually it is about an outrageous or funny interaction they just had with a customer (and often with a negative twist). Combat this subtle negativity with stories of your own. And since you were about to ask, here's what I recommend:

- **FIRST: Relay stories you hear** – As the leader of the department, you have access to customer comments. You also hear things from your peers and superiors that tell a positive story of performance. Share these!!! Either through e-mail, a poster board of accolades, ribbons at their desk, etc.
- **SECOND: Solicit stories** –Your staff has all kinds of great stories about service to customers and doing the right things. Ask them, then let everyone else know about them.
- **THIRD: Memorialize the stories** – Zappos creates a story book and most companies have a wall devoted to guest letters/comments. Whichever way you choose, you should put together the collection in a public place. That way, when things

are a little down, everyone has the collection of good stories to fall back on.

A culture of stories also helps you to better paint the picture down the road and helps you make better decisions. It lets you know where you have been, and gives you concrete evidence/experience of what has worked in the past and what resonates with the customer. These things are all just a bonus on top of maintaining control over the atmosphere in your department. So start putting story time into play, you'll be glad you did.

LESSON ASSIGNMENT: Start by coming up with a procedure for customer compliments. Maybe every one of them routes through you or a supervisor, maybe they are written down and submitted to a box to be drawn out, maybe there is a reward to encourage participation. Once you are able to gather these compliments and the stories that go along with them you can begin sharing and memorializing.

Little Gestures Go a Long Way

"If you're good to your staff when things are going well, they'll rally when times go bad." ~Mary Kay Ash

"The simple act of paying positive attention to people has a great deal to do with productivity." ~Tom Peters

· · · · ·

One of the most important things you do as a leader is to let your team know that they are important to you. However, as we all know, we don't always have the time to truly invest in the staff even when we know how important it is. So even though every leadership book screams "Spend More Time With Your People" we need to find a way to do so when we don't have the time for one-on-one's, team meetings, observations, etc. One of the ways around this conflict of priorities are to do the little things right...

- **Good morning and good night** – Get in the habit of saying good morning and good night to the team, usually they are either just starting or are wrapping up their day, so they are less inclined to get into a long conversation with you, and it lets everyone know when you are available and un-available.
- **Check in after their vacation or when they are sick** – One of the best things to do to show someone that they are important to you is to let them know that you noticed their absence.
- **Make sure they have the basic supplies to do their job** – It seems simple enough, and it really isn't anything that will score you points, but it will prevent points from being taken away. Whoever orders the basic supplies, pens, paper, tissue, post-it notes, better be sure to order a little extra to ensure you never run out. It's just the respectable thing to do for people who are important to you.
- **Water cooler chit chat** – Plan on stopping by the water cooler or break room for a drink every once in a while and ask how everyone's day is going. Usually you will get some pleasant conversations, and they understand if you need to cut it short and get back to work if it starts dragging on too long.
- **Take different ways to the bathroom, copier, etc** – Oftentimes there are areas of the department that you physically never set foot in based on your office location and the office setup. Take "the long way" a few times a week.
- **Buy them doughnuts once a month** – While I'm not in favor of buying your staff off with gifts, every once in a while (for no particular reason other than you wanted to do something for

them) go ahead and buy them some doughnuts, bagels, or pizza to show your appreciation.

These are just a few things that I have done to show my staff that I care, even though I don't always have time to show it in more traditional and time-intensive ways. Try these, try your own, but by all means try something to get some more time and presence with your staff.

LESSON ASSIGNMENT: Pick one of the above suggestions and integrate it into your workflow this week. After two weeks, add another one, then another two weeks after that, etc., etc.

Master the Message (Part 1 - Bad News)

"Take a method and try it. If it fails, admit it frankly, & try another. But by all means, try something." ~Franklin D. Roosevelt

"The first responsibility of a leader is to define reality. The last is to say thank you. In between, the leader is a servant." ~Max DePree

· · · · ·

When you need to convey something to your team, peer, or boss it is important that you "tailor" the way it is communicated in the way that best conveys your intended meaning. I'm not talking about "spinning" the message in a positive or negative way that detracts from the truth of the issue. What I am talking about is conveying it in the way that gets everything across that you want to get across (your intention with this communication). While it is important to do so with both good and bad news I think it is fair to say it is most important with bad news since the implications of bad news lend themselves to being passed along by the rumor mill.

Too often we have something to pass on and we just send out an e-mail by default. E-mail is quick and easy, but is the worst way to leverage your message as it is the poorest communication technique. So in an ideal setting, what should you strive for from a communication standpoint when delivering bad news?

- Always in person
    - They can see your body language and hear the inflection in your voice.
    - They can ask questions immediately.
    - *You* can see if they "get it".
- Always as quick as possible
    - "Bad news isn't wine, it doesn't improve with age" ~Colin Powell
    - Ensures that they don't find out from someone else so you can maintain control.
- Always let them know what you are doing about it.
    - The discussion then becomes constructive.
    - You can *show* them where the light at the end of the tunnel is.
    - If you weren't proactive in the avoidance of the issue, you can at least be proactive in the solution.
- If you can't do it in person, at least do it over the phone.
    - With the exception of body language (you and them) you have all of the other traits noted above.
- If you can't do it yourself, give it to a trusted Lieutenant.
    - Then follow up with the team yourself as soon as possible

Now this is what you should "strive" for. Obviously in today's workplace, you don't always have the time, but you do need to balance all of your interests and deliver as much impact as possible when you can. The idea is that you act quickly, take ownership, and plan the way out. Your plan should be to squash as much bad news right away so that there is nothing left to discuss but positive and constructive elements.

LESSON ASSIGNMENT: For the next month: When you have bad news do not send out an e-mail. Have a conversation over the phone or in person with the individuals involved or affected.

Master the Message (Part 2 – Good News)

"For a manager to be perceived as a positive manager, they need a four to one positive to negative contact ratio." ~Ken Blanchard

"Celebrate what you want to see more of." ~Tom Peters

· · · · ·

Bad news is something that we are all *very* used to managing because the pain of delivering it sticks in our mind, but what about the good news? Do you manage the good news to maximize the positive benefit on your department? Most of us don't, and if you are one of the many who don't you are missing and enormous opportunity to give your team more of a positive kick in the pants. Here is what I recommend:

- **"Own" your successes** – The biggest issue most of us face when mastering the message of good news is that we don't even talk about it. Too often we expect the success to happen, so we don't publicize it, or we feel like we are bragging. But as Drucker says above, we need *much more* positive messaging than negative messaging, so you must own the successes when they come so you can create the environment of positivity.

- **Pictures/Graphs** – Not everyone responds to speeches or memos. Really show the impact of the improvement by creating a pie chart, a graph, pictures, or something when you can. The more effort you put into it, the more people will recognize it.
  - Hint-Don't be afraid to adjust the scale to show maximum impact. Not all charts need to start at zero. A chart showing an increase from 70 to 80 that starts at zero and peaks at 100, doesn't "appear" to show as much improvement as one that starts from 60 and peaks at 100.
- **Shout it from the rooftops** – Make a big announcement, call it out in pre-shift, do something to make everyone aware of what took place. If you can't be sure that 100% of your staff is going to know about it, you aren't "shouting" loud enough.
- **Leverage the past success for the next success** – The real benefit is being able to shout out how good the news is to give you the political and emotional leverage to bring your team to the *next* level. A positive message should always end with what is next on the horizon to strive for.
- **Look for more of it** – You want to look for success in every corner you can find it so that you always have good things to talk about when needed.

So to sum up the last two chapters: Handling things in person, quickly and with a plan for the future are the keys to getting the most out of your news. You want to squash bad news by leaving nothing for further discussion, and leverage good news for the next thing.

LESSON ASSIGNMENT: Finding and thinking about success is often the first hurdle. Keep a list as the day progresses of all of the good news (no matter how small). Then report on all of these during a pre-shift meeting on the next morning.

Reach 10% and Effect 10% More

"As a leader, you're probably not doing a good job unless your employees can do a good impression of you when you're not around." ~Patrick Lencioni

"Leadership is not just what happens when you're there, it's what happens when you're not there." ~Ken Blanchard

. . . . .

I try to remind myself of this whenever I think about giving just a little less to a conversation I have with an employee. As a leader, you are constantly in the spotlight and are constantly under very high expectations from your staff (at least they should have high expectations of you). Many times we consider this a burden, but it is also an opportunity to have our good deeds magnified as the stories of your management are told from one employee to another. Your team is going to talk about you, so give them something good to talk about. Some thoughts on this:

- **Use the grapevine** - You don't need to mention it to every employee when there are some small issues (dress code, a few minutes late from lunch, etc). Oftentimes you can come down on a few and they will tell the rest. This is a classic 80/20 proposition, where for 20% of the effort of reaching everyone, you get 80% of the benefit. Caution: if it is of importance, then you *need* to reach out to the 100%.
- **Find the influential employees** – When looking to use the grapevine, it is obviously best to utilize the "social butterflies" in your group. But with that said, you must balance that out as you

do not want to be perceived as having favorites, or if it is bad news, employees you are targeting.

- **Make a connection** – It is when things are most stressful that you have the best opportunity to make that impact, positively or negatively. The employee has a last minute vacation request, has a death in the family, is having a real problem with the new material, has an irate customer they need help with, etc. It is during these times where they will truly appreciate any extra effort you put forth…..and that is where you will make the biggest connection.
- **Flipping causes disruption** – This can be good and bad. If you have a bad reputation amongst your staff, flipping and being more understanding or informed will be a change that warrants discussion amongst the staff. Likewise, if you are a great leader and you are having a tough day, then that negativity will also be a change that causes the staff to talk. So either use the change for your benefit, or as a cautionary tale.

People talk, and we work in a human environment so the grapevine will exist anywhere, but that doesn't need to be a bad thing. If you use it well, it can actually be a big help to you both in workload and message.

LESSON ASSIGNMENT: The first thing to do is to determine who are the most influential and talkative members of your team. This should not be more than 10% of your staff. This week you need to go around and have a positive conversation about the performance of the organization or department with each one of these individuals.

Step Up Before Your Employees Step Down

The Manager's Diary II

Great Talent

Hard to Find & Tough to Develop

The Manager's Diary II

Don't Be Your Own Worst Enemy When Hiring

"You're only as good as the people you hire." ~Ray Kroc

"Hire people who are better than you are, then leave them to get on with it". ~David Ogilvy

· · · · ·

One of the biggest mistakes in hiring is settling for a candidate who will "probably do just fine" instead of holding out for a great addition to your team. It's a natural thing that I have fallen into from time to time in my career, and comes about for a few common reasons:

- **Not enough candidates** – "Really, we're done? You don't have anyone else?"
- **Not enough time to interview** – "Seriously! Can't we just get this over with? I have better things to do."
- **Interview fatigue** – "I've done 50 interviews this week. I swear to heaven I will hire the next person who walks through the door!"
- **Not clear on what you want** – "Well he has some of the things we're looking for???"

Yes, you may find a candidate who can do the job, but you're looking for a candidate that can do the job *very* well. While this article is not meant to tackle any of the root causes of the above, I wanted to acknowledge them to highlight some of the main areas where we all struggle in interviewing. One criteria to use when trying to keep yourself focused on only hiring the right candidates, while allowing some flexibility is this:

"Does this employee raise the average for talent amongst your employee pool?"

By focusing on obtaining employees better than your current employees you reduce the tendency to settle, and even if you do find a way to settle a little, at that point you probably have an average employee (as opposed to the below average disaster you may have ended up with). When your staff sees great talent coming on board it focuses them on meeting the "challenge" of keeping up, but on a positive side, instills in them a pride that this person chose to work for your organization. There is a halo effect amongst your team when there is a perception that only "great talent" works in the organization.

So try this out when making your next hiring decision. I find it to be a simple way of ensuring I don't settle and keep the talent trajectory in my department heading in the right direction.

LESSON ASSIGNMENT: Clarity is something that is critical in hiring. What are the job responsibilities? Who are you looking for? What skills must they have? So keep in mind one other thing: Who is a team member of yours that performs the job to an average degree of proficiency in comparison to their peers? Now once you have that answer, ask yourself the question in the interview, "Are they better than _____."

Have You Identified Your Successor

"The growth and development of people is the highest calling of leadership." ~Harvey S. Firestone

"When opportunity comes, it's too late to prepare." ~John Wooden

· · · · ·

You can't move on in your career until an opportunity is opened or created for you (or preferably by you). However, there is also a second thing; whether there is someone to take your place. Usually the opportunity above you trumps any inconvenience having you leave your current position creates, so your boss will usually still pull the trigger. But what if they don't? What if it is an opportunity that *you* would like to seize, but your boss isn't too keen on? What if you're leaving the organization and this would burn a bridge? Then what? Or possibly, what if your organization would like to temporarily give you some experience and exposure in another area? Are you prepared to let someone take the reins? Have you prepared them to succeed? If you haven't, don't feel bad, succession planning is something that is put off by the most seasoned of Executives. But that just means you are in an illustrious group of people who need to *get to work*. Luckily getting started and on your way is relatively simple:

- **What skills do they need to be successful?** What are the tasks they need to do, skills they need to have, and the behaviors they need to exhibit? Make the list.
- **Who has them?** Who is demonstrating some of the above *now*? If they aren't exhibiting *some* of the traits then they probably should not be in the running.

- **Who has the potential to have them all?** You need to work with a person who has the ability to be as successful as possible.
- **When can you give them some exposure?** Now that you have selected possible successors, give them as much exposure as possible to prepare them. Vacations are a great chance to give them ownership while you are gone. Meetings are also great opportunities for you to pass along some real world experience. Even better, delegate a task to them so there is less for them to learn when you get your promotion and they move up.

One of the first things to have these candidates do is to help you put together the procedure manual for everything that you do from a reporting, evaluation, and decision standpoint. If you're an aspiring Supervisor, make sure that whatever special duties you have are backed up by someone else. Often you have a task that you handle for a member of management (hopefully because they have identified you as a successor) that will need to be handled by someone else when you move up the ladder. Make sure you have documentation and have shown a person or two how to do it.

Don't leave succession planning to chance. Eventually it will slow your career progression.

LESSON ASSIGNMENT: It is best to identify more than one possible candidate. If your department is smaller, try to find two and if it is a larger department shoot for three people. Any more than three people and you may struggle to keep them all engaged. Then start assigning tasks and giving them exposure and see who steps up and starts shining.

Learn From the Routine

"Sometimes the best way to learn is to return to the fundamentals." ~John Maxwell

"Leadership and learning are indispensable to each other." ~John Fitzgerald Kennedy

· · · · ·

Often overlooked, the basics are ripe for the picking when looking to improve performance in your staff. Six Sigma and other continuous improvement structures often look to the basic and the routine because small changes have *big* impact when repeated 100+ times during the day. People, tools, and the business environment change, and so can their application. The longer it has been since you have reviewed basic job functions of your staff, the better the chance that you can find improvements.

Not sold on the idea of reviewing all of the basic tasks of your staff yet? Consider these thoughts:

- **The basics are your foundation** - The better your foundation is the more opportunities for growth you have and the more time you have to focus on higher value tasks. If you can't efficiently satisfy the basic needs of your customer, no other work matters
- **Promotes a culture of learning and change** – "If they are looking to improve *that*, then what about…" The current

business environment is very fluid, and those organizations that are able to constantly seek an edge will be more competitive. Stagnation in people, product, or process spells death to any modern business.

- **Teaches *mastery*** - Just like anything you start small then grow. Start small by mastering the basics, as your staff becomes experts at the basics you can use that success to build mastery in the more important tasks and functions.

Some may say that reviewing the basics isn't as interesting as working on "forward looking" initiatives. But if you can get the basics right you free up time to work on those things and you lay a strong foundation that will allow you to build higher. And *that is* interesting for almost any of us.

LESSON ASSIGNMENT: Take a look at one basic function a week, maybe in a small focus group or maybe shadowing. Do it with three routine tasks and I bet you find something worthwhile to improve operations. Like I say, try it for three weeks straight and see.

Let Your Staff Vote on Stuff

"In the past a leader was a boss. Today leaders must be partners with their people. They no longer can lead based on positional power." ~Ken Blanchard

"Good leaders make people feel that they're at the very heart of things, not at the periphery." ~Warren Bennis

Step Up Before Your Employees Step Down

. . . . .

Employee Engagement is a very popular topic right now in management circles with a huge number of articles espousing its benefits and importance. One way that I have used to get my staff involved and engaged is to let them vote on things, some of which are important and some more frivolous: Things like customer correspondence templates, whether to split lunch breaks or keep them together, dress code questions, when our next Pot Luck should be and what the theme is. Doing so has a host of benefits for overall morale and culture, but there are a few considerations on your part.

- **All options must be "legal and approved"** - There is no sense voting on an option that HR won't sign off on or that the Finance Department won't back. So get the approvals ahead of time, otherwise it could be demoralizing to the team.
- **You must be OK with the options** – Similar to the above you must be willing to get behind whichever option is chosen. For this reason I prefer to vet the choices before sending it out to the team, this maintains a certain level of control. With that said, remember that you don't have a monopoly on the best ideas, so even things that you aren't sure would work should be included. Give the team a chance to change your mind.
- **You *can* impeach the winning vote at a later date (with good cause)** – Collective decisions usually get ahead of problems down the road as there are more people looking at it. But if it is evident that what was chosen isn't working after you have put it into place for a while, you can absolutely change. Just be sure to let the team know why you are making the change and the issues that are leading to it.

Depending how your team reacts to this, you may find them voting on policies and procedures more and more often. To do so keeps them engaged, gives them ownership of the department and their work, and increases adoption. Start voting on the simple and frivolous things first, then start rolling out increasingly important choices to the team. In the end you may be surprised on the issues that end up being "put to a vote".

LESSON ASSIGNMENT: Look at your calendar and your "to-do list." Pick three things that you can safely put to a vote with your team. There should be many more things than that, but let's start with three. Then send out an e-mail asking for ideas on the three items and pull everyone together for a discussion and a vote the next day.

Leverage the New Hires for Excitement

"One person with passion is better than forty people merely interested." ~E. M. Forster

"The wildest colts make the best horses." ~Plutarch

. . . . .

Complacency is something that needs to be battled in any department that has been around for a while. One of the ways to battle the "humdrum, same old same old" mentality is to use the people that are most excited about working for you....your new hires! Your new hires are as high as a kite when they first come on board, so keep them there and use that enthusiasm to give your entire team a shot in the arm.

First you need to manage the integration of them into the existing team. A couple of ideas to make their transition complete, productive and contagious:

- **Find out about them** - Have them fill out a questionnaire and have every existing team member fill it out as well to find out about their background, passions, and anything else. Then publish to the entire team so that everyone can see what makes them tick. This helps build unique bonds between team members.
- **Have them select their trainer** - Create resumes and report cards for your departmental trainers, reward trainers for their involvement so that they are excited about the opportunity, then line them up like an elementary school kickball team and have the newbies "draft" them.
- **Play a game and/or have them reach milestones** - Perhaps they can't graduate until they sell $1,000 in merchandise in a day, open 10 accounts in a week, or have 3 days in a row without an error. Do something fun that has a positive impact and focuses the new hires on what they need to do, and brings the rest of the team into it (make sure to publish results for everyone to see)

Once the new-hires have graduated, give them prominent exposure in the organization. Too often we leverage our most senior people because of their knowledge and experience, but rarely do these people have the most passion in the department. Treat your new hires like your most senior people and put them front and center in the operation. If you are really concerned about whether they are ready, give them a lieutenant from among your more senior people. You may be surprised at the ideas and energy that come up:

- Have them run a meeting
- Have them head a project
- Give them some function to "own" in your department

Give your team a boost, improve your overall enthusiasm and morale, and use the fire from the newbies to rekindle your own. Once they are trained and integrated into your team, you may find that they are some of your best employees and lift the others to new heights, but this won't happen until you recognize and leverage the opportunity.

LESSON ASSIGNMENT: Put together a questionnaire this week for everyone to fill out. Simple questions are the least threatening and open the door to further communication. A few suggestions; number of siblings, how many cities have they lived in, favorite food, least favorite food, favorite vacation spot, etc. Once you have everyone fill it out, call a meeting and have everyone go over theirs. When you have new-hires come on board go through the same process each time with similar or different questions.

Step Up Before Your Employees Step Down

The Manager's Diary II

Yourself

If You Can't Manage Yourself, You're In Trouble

The Manager's Diary II

It Only Takes Two Seconds to be a Better Leader

"I can give you a six-word formula for success: Think things through - then follow through." ~Edward Rickenbacker

"Being busy is a form of laziness—lazy thinking and indiscriminate action." ~Tim Ferris

• • • • •

As leaders we are all crazy busy. We have a ton on our plate and not enough time to tackle even a portion of what is on it. But like any pressure it can create cracks that create the chance for mistakes and problems. It makes us hurry, it makes us short-tempered, and it makes us prone to quick decisions. None of these are traits we want to see take root. So what to do?

I recommend one simple and small step in the right direction: *Take one breath before responding to a question….all it takes is two seconds.*

- **Two seconds** help us to pause and think, thus giving a less reflexive and better thought out answer
- **Two seconds** (and a deep breath) help us calm down, thus lengthening the fuse on our temper
- **Two seconds** helps our staff members finish their question, thus showing them respect
- **Two seconds** represents a pause in the day to help us de-stress

We all know many bosses who cut their staff off with the answer to a question that hasn't fully been asked. They are the same ones who seem to be quick to anger and making impulsive decisions. Don't be one of them. Take a breath, take a couple of seconds, and take a step toward being an even better leader.

LESSON ASSIGNMENT: Start without the need for it. Breathing is something that we take for granted. Set a recurring meeting on your calendar labeled "one breath" and schedule it every 15 minutes throughout the day. Do this the whole day and you'll be more conscious of it and be able to roll it out into practice the following day.

Great Leaders Laugh at Work

"There is little success where there is little laughter." ~Andrew Carnegie

"A well-developed sense of humor is the pole that adds balance to your steps as you walk the tightrope of life." ~William Arthur Ward

. . . . .

In our day to day work life we are constantly beset with troubles and challenges. If we are not too careful our job becomes serious at best, and tedious at worst. It is for this reason that every great leader has the ability to use humor at correct moments to get more out of his/her team. This can come to pass by laughing at our own mistakes, making light of the troubles we face, or simply sharing humorous stories from the weekend.

Step Up Before Your Employees Step Down

But beyond blowing off steam, there are a number of other reasons to let a little humor into your leadership style:

- **Approachability** – By engaging with your staff in a lighthearted way, you increase your approachability which is necessary for you to be up to date on challenges and successes in the department.
- **Creativity** – Humor breaks up the monotony and gets our minds out of the rut we find ourselves in when doing our daily tasks. It is these breaks in thinking that often lead to new ideas and solutions.
- **Reduces Stress** – It's hard to be stressed out when you're laughing, and stress in the workplace is no good for morale, health or teamwork.
- **Increases Productivity** – If you're having fun at work, your tasks tend to flow quicker and with more precision. As a leader, you're also apt to have less turnover if your staff is enjoying themselves.

One thing that I have instituted recently in an effort to insert a little humor into the day is a daily joke (a clean joke) that I e-mail to the staff in the middle of the day. I think sending it in the middle of the day is the best way to get the most out of the points listed above. This direct approach may work for some of you, for others it may be just as much about demeanor. The other suggestion is any group gathering. People *want* to laugh and have fun, so if you get them together outside of the work setting (and the lunchroom counts) you'll be likely to reap some of the benefits of a good atmosphere.

Regardless of the approach you take, I hope you will consider the importance of at least a little laughter in the workplace.

LESSON ASSIGNMENT: How are you going to institute laughter? If you don't have any idea of your own, go ahead and steal on of the above. The key is that you start right away, so get ready to Google "jokes."

Fresh Air for Fresh Ideas

"Anyone's life truly lived consists of work, sunshine, exercise, soap, plenty of fresh air, and a happy contented spirit." ~Lilly Langtry

"True enjoyment comes from activity of the mind and exercise of the body; the two are united." ~Alexander von Humboldt

. . . . .

The next time you need to meet with a couple of colleagues to do some brainstorming on a problem or come up with an idea, walk right past the conference room and out the door! Take a walk through the warehouse, a walk in the park next door, a walk around the building, or a walk around the block. Here's why:

- Breaking the monotonous rut is a key to creativity. And sadly, getting outside or in different areas of your building is actually breaking habitual behavior since we are creatures of routine.
- From a physiological standpoint, by moving around you'll increase the flow of blood to your brain. Never a bad thing when you're looking to use it!
- If you need to memorialize anything you can do so by taking a note or e-mailing from your smartphone. If someone has an iPad or Tablet, this could be a great way to use it.

Another trick to this is to immediately get to work on the problem or new idea when you get back to your desk. This allows you to take any momentum from your "walkabout" and translate that into the issue at hand and the rest of the day. I recommend this because sometimes the transition from outside movement to inside sitting kills any momentum you may have had in your day.

But don't limit this to brainstorming sessions. I have had one on one meetings take place while walking around the block, I've met with an outside vendor while walking through our facility, and even if I can't escape the conference room, I will look to use another department's conference room to at least change up which paintings I'm looking at on the wall.

So get out, move around, and you'll find you are more creative and more positive. I dare you to try it and find any different.

LESSON ASSIGNMENT: Take three meetings on your calendar next week and schedule them in a different location than you have before. This can be another meeting room, a different department, or even outside.

How to Be a Know It All at Work

"The secret of business is to know something that nobody else knows." ~Aristotle Onassis

"Leadership and learning are indispensable to each other." ~John Fitzgerald Kennedy

. . . . .

One of best pieces of advice I ever received was to "look over the shoulder" of those you rely on when they are working on nor fixing something for you and your department. By looking over their shoulder, you learn how to fix the mistake yourself next time (if you have the access and the tools), convey better information the next time something goes wrong, and let someone else know exactly what is wrong and what needs to be done when it happens to them (how valuable are you to your peers now?).

Now the "look over the shoulder" method in no way makes you an expert in any particular area, however, it does add to the number of tools you can call upon to get through your day easier, or just as importantly, gives you a clearer picture of how things work which makes your decision making more precise. And these are two goals that every single one of us should have at the front of our minds. So how do we put the "look over the shoulder" technique to work?

- **Make time for it** – Too often we leave the I.T. representative to fix our computer while we go get coffee, the sales representative to set up the display while we tend to other matters, the construction workers to do their work while we go back to our office, but what could we learn if we stuck around for at least a little while? The answer: sometimes a lot and sometimes not so much, but you'll never learn anything if you never set foot in the classroom. So commit to learning at least a little, I've seen VP's and CEO's stick around to watch someone do their work, or to ask them some relatively simple questions about it, and you should too. It takes a little time out of our day, but as referenced above, it is time that matches our goals.

- **Focus and don't focus** – Focus on what is being done that directly affects your work, but also broaden your focus to see how the work can give you a better understanding of the whole system. How what the I.T. guy is doing for your one problem could be used to help with other problems, how the Sales Rep's approach to his product could help sales in other categories, and how the construction workers project fits in with others. This is the step that leverages specific knowledge for broader purposes.
- **Ask questions** – Probably one of the most important keys is to ask questions while they work. Typically they are good enough to do their job and give you insight at the same time that lets you keep up. This is also where you can work on your "broadening" of knowledge as mentioned above:
    - "So could you use this technique in any situation like this?"
    - "How would you do this, if you needed to do _____?"
    - "What would you do if _____?"
- **Write it down** – Considering that these things are most likely not in your specific job description, I've always found that taking 30-60 seconds to write down my knowledge both cements it in my mind better, and also gives me a point of reference if I need to come back to it (checklists are especially good).

In today's environment, we are required to have a deeper knowledge of our particular duties. What this has done is make the "Jack of all Trades" even more rare and valuable (assuming they still maintain that deep knowledge of their work). If you want to be that "Go-To Person" in your department, and show your value to the organization in different ways than your peers, try looking over the shoulder of your support structure. The next time they aren't there to help, you may be there to save the day.

LESSON ASSIGNMENT: One scenario that all of us can relate to is when we have a computer problem. Next time stick around and watch what the IT guru is doing and ask questions about what happened and how he/she is fixing it. After doing this a few times I'll be willing to bet there will be a couple of things you'll be able to fix yourself from now on.

Get in the Habit of Turning Off Your Smartphone

"When people talk, listen completely. Most people never listen." ~Ernest Hemingway

"The simple act of paying positive attention to people has a great deal to do with productivity" ~Tom Peters

. . . . .

There is a lot of talk about how our "always on" culture is breaking down our ability to focus, our personal relationships, and even our health. A general rule that I believe is beneficial on this topic, as with most others, is to seek moderation. The best way to find moderation with something as ubiquitous as this is to be specific, and seek out "high value" instances of use or disuse.

In the case of your smartphone in particular, I think there can be three specific areas of "high value" benefit. These are listed in decreasing order of acceptance in our culture:

- **Meetings** – In many organizations there is already a "turn off your phone" policy for meetings, however, it is usually only sporadically adhered to. So what would you gain by turning off your phone? Well the first one is that you'd never have to utter that embarrassing phrase "I'm sorry, could you repeat that?" (don't tell me you haven't said that before). But beyond that:
  - *Others would know you respect them enough to give them your full attention* (would you answer e-mail on your phone when meeting with the CEO? Probably not). This means they are more apt to pay full attention when you are presenting.
  - *You can focus on the purpose of the meeting.* If you are engaged, you can be a part of the solution or direction of the meeting subject. I believe half the reason most meetings are a waste of time is that nobody is fully engaged in the topic.
  - *You can learn from others.* Whether it be how they think through a problem, areas within their operation you can be of assistance in, or simply finding out more about your colleagues and their departments (always important background)
- **One on one meetings** – Take the meeting out of your office and away from your computer. Make it in a meeting room. Again, you show the person respect by focusing on them and not the latest distraction. But even more important than that, you show how much you respect the *content* of the meeting. Giving feedback is one of the most important things we do as leaders and it's essential that we convey the importance of what we are providing our team.
- **Lunches** – The least "socially acceptable" of the three is to turn off your phone during lunches. I personally find that the break in the day allows me some time for free thinking, possibly de-stress a little, and come back to tackle problems with fresh energy and a fresh perspective.

Smartphones are amazing tools and have made communication easier and timelier, but just like any tool, they aren't always best used in every task you have. We can all get away for 30 minutes without raising too much discontent amongst others, so start now. Whether it is focusing on the task at hand without distraction or allowing yourself time to recharge or brainstorm, it is time *very* well spent for you and the organization you serve.

LESSON ASSIGNMENT: See how many meetings you can go through this week without looking at your smartphone. A tip: Keep it in your pocket so you aren't even tempted to look at it.

Are You an Ambidextrous Leader

"It is a mistake to look too far ahead. Only one link in the chain of destiny can be handled at a time." ~ Winston Churchill

"The most successful business people hold onto the old just as long as it's good & grab the new just as soon as it's better." ~Lee Iacocca

• • • • •

One of the things that slows progress for many departments and businesses is that they are so focused on improving their operation/product with the latest and greatest thing that they begin neglecting their core business and duties while they bring the next thing to market. It is a totally understandable occurrence, as proper change management and/or innovation requires an enormous amount of focus, and that can be difficult if not impossible to split equally between your existing role and your work on the future. This results in a "two steps forward, one step back" dance, as you often immediately need to go back and clean up what was neglected in the operation as soon as you are done with the improvement.

So how do we ensure that our department makes steady progress forward? A few things:

- **"Lock in" what you have established already** – Do you have the Standard Operating Procedures written? Have you clearly established ownership of the product/service? Are you crystal clear on what metrics will be reviewed and what they should look like? This is the cleanup that should take place beforehand.
- **Set the course for the old process/product** – What are your expectations and goals for the current process while you are working on "the next big thing"? Are there enhancement timelines to hit, are there service goals, sales goals, etc? Point the direction you want the ship to go before you jump over to navigate the next ship. Make sure the team is clear on purpose. This helps the department run without you.
- **Make time to review and meet** – It is very tempting to be engrossed in the new project. Schedule a few minutes each day to review the metrics discussed above (hence why we needed to be clear on them) and then a few more minutes to check in on the personnel. This status check will ensure that things are still progressing with the "old" while you bring on the "new". I recommend the beginning of the morning before getting engrossed in other things.

By managing your focus and getting clear on expectations/metrics you can ensure that current operations are "locked in" and won't erode as you start moving resources to the next improvement for your organization/department.

LESSON ASSIGNMENT: Do you have any processes in your department that are "locked in" or that run on auto-pilot? Ask what you have done right with that process and roll it out to others so that you free up time and energy for yourself to improve the operation. If you don't have any processes that fit that description then start with the questions prior.

Can't Play Until You've Eaten Your Vegetables

"Discipline is doing what you really do not want to do, so you can do what you really want to do." ~John C. Maxwell

"When you have a number of disagreeable duties to perform, always do the most disagreeable first." ~Josiah Quincy

. . . . .

We all want to do the wild and crazy things that change the world of our organization, those are the fun things that highlight how much we can contribute to the greater good of the organization. But we were hired or promoted to run the day to day of a department or division first. If we are not careful, the day to day management of our department can get away from us while we work on our "pet" projects, and eventually lead to problems.

Now I am a big proponent of all employees spending time working on the organization's biggest problems, but there is a time and place for everything. As the title of the chapter indicates, you have to take care of your "primary" job duties first, before you start tackling other things. But don't fret, there are a few tricks that I have learned in a long career of tackling my job duties *and* tackling issues in other departments or the corporate level. The main thing is to: *Manage your time and focus*. You can do that easiest with a few ideas:

- **First thing in the morning get ahead of your vegetables** – The quicker you eat your vegetables, the quicker you can move on to more savory food. Like having dinner before dessert, you *must* tackle your departmental job duties right from the get-go. This also allows you to get as many things started and toward completion as possible, leaving the potential for downtime later that can be spent on things that are more fun.
- ***Define* moments during the day when you can play** – Schedule provides structure. Finite amounts of time during the day restrict you from spending the "whole afternoon" on something other than your primary job focus. They also focus your efforts during that time.
- **Take notes of thoughts you can come back to** – Writing down ideas or thoughts gets them out of your head until you are ready to properly deal with them. This has also served me well when coming up with ideas for my day in day out duties. You can focus on what you are doing at the time, then come back and focus on the idea later. For me, I just e-mail myself to memorialize it.
- **The end of the day is yours** – Take care of your business during the day, and whatever time is left over at the end of your day is yours to do with as you please.

So by all means, have fun tackling the biggest problems in the organization. Just make sure you have taken care of your work first.

LESSON ASSIGNMENT: Schedule one hour on Wednesday or Thursday afternoon to consider big things. Why Wednesday and Thursday? Well Monday and Tuesday are usually spent getting some momentum behind things you want to accomplish over the week and issues you thought more about over the weekend. And Friday is usually set aside for finishing things off and task clean-up. But also schedule one hour at the beginning of each of those days to focus on regular duties and tasks that you need to get accomplished.

The Enemy of Management: The Grey Area

"A clear vision, backed by definite plans, gives you a tremendous feeling of confidence and personal power." ~Brian Tracy

"When your values are clear to you, making decisions becomes easier." ~Roy E. Disney

. . . . .

"Keep your friends close, but your enemies closer" is an old quote and in this case it is just as applicable for leaders operating in their departments. In this case, the enemy is the "grey area" where things are not as clear as they could/should be. While you need to be aware of the areas in your operation where things are clear, it is in the unclear areas where you need to get up close and personal. It is in these "grey areas" where potential problems lie, and sometimes some catastrophic ones at that. You simply cannot manage areas of your organization effectively when you can't see clearly what is occurring.

While the "grey areas" are endless in a business of any size, I want to speak about two of the most impactful and potentially dangerous grey areas where you want to stay closely involved:

- **Grey Ownership** – Do you have clear owners of each one of your processes and products? If not, this is now a grey area where nobody owns it. So in each area/task where you identify no ownership, set ownership. This is most tricky on cross-departmental things, and that is why you need to be aware and get with the leader in the other department and set dual owners or a single owner in one of the departments. It's too easy to play the blame game when collaboration doesn't work out as expected.
- **Grey Expectations** – Are you clear on what you are asking? What end result you are looking for? What deadline has been established? If not, or more likely, if you are not certain that the other party has understood, go ahead and ensure that they are. Write it down and follow-up, sometimes people will sabotage a task by simply working within the "grey area" and saying "I didn't know you expected *that*." Don't let that happen to you.

If everything was clear, most businesses wouldn't need half of the managers they have (so thank goodness there is grey area). But that is the environment we need to live in, bringing clarity to unclear situations.

LESSON ASSIGNMENT: Focus on getting clear on ownership and expectations this week, and count the number of times where there was going to be a miscommunication that created a problem. That will give you the evidence to keep pushing for clarity in the future.

The Big Picture is for Perspective not Excuses

"Everyone is against micro managing but macro managing means you're working at the big picture but don't know the details." ~Henry Mintzberg

"Never neglect details. When everyone's mind is dulled or distracted the leader must be doubly vigilant." ~Colin Powell

. . . . .

A crutch that many companies, departments and leaders use is to take the "10,000 foot view" not to gain perspective, but to hide failings in the business or to excuse underperformance. Almost everything looks better from a distance. The common adage of "Don't miss the forest through the trees" is absolutely true, but you need the proper mix of detail and high level. A couple of typical excuses attempting to use the big picture:

- *"Well that was only one customer"* – The correct response: Only one customer that you know about. Studies show that only one in every ten dissatisfied customers will complain. And isn't one unhappy customer still an issue?
- *"We receive four out of five stars on our reviews"* – The correct response: But how many one and two star reviews have you received, and why? There is an issue just waiting to be addressed there.

The above two examples highlight an overly simplified viewpoint that is quickly refuted. Leaders who use the big picture as an excuse tend to try to put their issue into the largest pool possible to dilute its impact (a handful of dirt has no effect on a swimming pool, but turns a glass full of water to mud). Department managers are responsible for the details, and in larger departments, have Supervisors who can get even more granular with things. For them, the important perspective isn't the big picture, it is *in the details*.

Another common occurrence is the "bench player syndrome" where an underperforming member of the team (or organization) considers their performance excusable because the entire team (or organization) is doing well. In the big picture, overall performance is great, but that doesn't mean you have a team of All-Stars. These people try to blend in with the success around them, and are usually exposed when things take any sort of turn for the worse.

The question to ask in all of this is: *Are you excelling at what you control?* If you aren't, then focus on the problem, not how it isn't "that big of a problem in the grand scheme of things". If you focus on addressing the problem, you will be rewarded with quicker and greater success and security.

LESSON ASSIGNMENT: Get specific with your operation. Take what you do best and what you do worst. Now put together three actions you can take to improve each of them. Make the best even better and raise the worst up a few notches. Put those actions on a timeline and set what the expected result is going to be. The big picture is great, but it is in the details that it moves forward.

Don't Be So Smart You're Stupid – Part 1

"Make sure your worst enemy doesn't live between your own two ears." ~Laird Hamilton

"Simplicity is the ultimate sophistication" -Leonardo da Vinci

. . . . .

Business is complex and difficult enough without any added degree of difficulty included. Too often we find ourselves making the routine things that we do "interesting", or tweaking things of little importance in an effort to move the operation forward. The way we do this is usually to make the task or project larger, more complicated, and more time consuming. Now gaining insight and increasing the impact of operations *are* good goals for the most part, the trouble comes in when they don't reach those goals, and instead add time and complexity without gaining much insight or impact.

Simplifying procedures, goals and operations while increasing productivity and visibility is one of the best things you can do as a leader. It frees up time to work on other things and helps you see things clearer. But let there be no doubt, there is a constant struggle with complexity as you attempt new things to improve operations. Believe it or not, complexity is often easier than simplicity *and* obviously shows that you are doing a *whole* bunch of work, which usually makes your boss proud.

What we need to strive for is that once something proves valuable, we simplify the process of creation and maintenance instead of adding things that prove to be of little value. Unfortunately we often feel a pull to hold on to the wasted time of valueless practices, which leaves us no time to simplify processes.

The example I use most often are reports utilizing Excel: They typically start small, then after a few meetings, a few months, and a few "could you add this to the report" it becomes a 90 minute ordeal each time you need to prepare it. The report is a success, but it has just become a burden. Since telling your boss or his/her peers that they can't have what they want isn't the best idea for your career, you need to find a new solution (here's where it is initially difficult to make things simple). The one that I have used are database and Excel gurus in the organization to automate the report. Now instead of 90 minutes, it takes 30 seconds to click "Refresh", but it took hours of time and effort that nobody saw to get there.

Sometimes you don't have the resources, or they are already busy filling their day with items that don't have much value (sorry, couldn't help a little playful cynicism). But if you can find the time to automate portions of the report, you can gain time in the future. Let's do a simple calculation. Let's say you can automate parts of the report mentioned above and reduce the time for preparation to only 30 minutes instead of 90 minutes. Now let's say it is going to take you 10 hours to make the changes, automate, and test. In this case if you do this report daily, you start coming out ahead after only two weeks. Then you can use the extra hour a day to automate and simplify even more things. The same calculation can be used with any process. Saving ten minutes every day saves almost an hour a week.

LESSON ASSIGNMENT: As you are improving operations, cut those things that bring no value and automate/streamline those that do add value as soon as you reap some success. This keeps the operation simple and clean and leaves more time to find the next improvement.

Don't Be So Smart You're Stupid – Part 2

"Make sure your worst enemy doesn't live between your own two ears." ~Laird Hamilton

"Simplicity is the ultimate sophistication" -Leonardo da Vinci

. . . . .

We have a bad tendency in management to make processes bigger and more complex than they need to be. Often we do this because it makes us feel more important and/or justifies how important we are. We know that our focus should be on productivity, but we do succumb to human nature occasionally. In the prior chapter I talked about how the implementation and experimenting with new processes should be streamlined to create greater simplicity and reduce clutter. In this chapter, I want to talk about *existing* procedures and the importance of continuously simplifying processes.

The power of simplicity is immense:

- **Less errors** – A reduction of complexity leaves less room for errors to be made. Automation reduces this even further by eliminating the possibility of error.
- **Speedier** – Simple usually means faster (not always) and faster means more time for the complex. Speedier can also reference how much faster people can be trained on a simple task vs. a complex one.
- **Easier to change processes** – In the ever changing business environment, it's important to be able to make tweaks to how

you conduct business. If there are less moving parts, there are fewer things to prepare.
- **Better accountability** – In a simple operation the owners are usually few and the dependencies are just as few. Without complexity the excuses for non-performance diminish.

OK, so you're sold on the benefits, and you've checked your ego at the door. So how do you make changes to operations that are already running? There are four ways and I will list them in degree of difficulty from easiest to hardest.

- **Eliminate** – Eliminating tasks that are of little value or add no value is the easiest way to make processes simpler. If you take a process from 10 steps to 8 steps, you've reduced the clutter and increased the speed associated with taking something from start to finish.
- **Reduce** – Do tasks less frequently. Maybe it is once a week instead of daily, or quarterly instead of monthly.
- **Automate** – The next step is to automate as many tasks as possible. This can be done with enhancements to the systems, the spreadsheets or processes surrounding them. The other way is to reuse material. If someone else is producing something, maybe they can make a small tweak that makes it easily useful for you.
- **Redesign** – The most difficult is process redesign, where you rethink how something is done to streamline it for all of the above noted reasons. You can segment tasks into specific specialties, utilize new resources/technology, and generally change it to fit how things run now as opposed to how they were done in the past.

The creation of simpler and simpler processes for your team begins a "virtuous loop" where you can use the time and effort saved to make other things simpler, and use that time to make them even simpler, etc. etc. It is these virtuous loops that eventually lead to incredible performance.

LESSON ASSIGNMENT: Let's free up some time! Find three duties that your Supervisors or team do that either don't need to be done or provide little value. Now stop doing them. Next, find three duties that your Supervisors or team do every day that could be done twice a week instead. Look at that! You've just freed up a bunch of time that was going towards "marginally" productive tasks that can be directed to more important things.

What is Your Worst Habit

"My troubles and obstacles, have strengthened me... a kick in the teeth may be the best thing in the world for you." ~Walt Disney

"Leaders are more powerful role models when they learn than when they teach" ~Rosabeth Moss Kantor

. . . . .

What if you could eliminate your greatest weakness? Public speaking, anger management, procrastination? How would that improve you career and your life? We usually try to avoid our weaknesses whenever possible. In fact, there is a philosophy about leveraging strengths instead of focusing on weaknesses, but as with everything you need balance between working on strengths and weaknesses. You don't get better at something by avoiding it, you get better at it by acknowledging it and coming up with a plan to work on it. Doing so is empowering and immediately begins mitigating the effects of the poor habit. But before you tackle your absolute worst trait, I recommend you try this "out of the box" idea first:

Don't decide what you biggest weakness is yourself…..ask your staff

What we may think is the worst thing isn't actually the most impactful weakness, and often we even hide our weaknesses from ourselves. Once you have a weakness to tackle, then start working on it:

- **Lessons** – Are there classes you can take if it is a skill or behavior. Sign up for some. Isn't the benefit of not having that weakness *well worth* the investment of time and possibly money?
- **Role Models** – Are there people that are *excellent* where you are weak? Seek them out and start working more closely with them.
- **Plan & Timetable** – Regardless of how you decide to get there, make a plan and set a timetable for accomplishing your goal. Set reasonable and reachable milestones along the way and get to work.

Sometimes you need to tackle things head on. If you've known about and talked about how you need to be better in an area for more than a year (many of us go a decade or more) then *fix it*. You have the power to do so.

LESSON ASSIGNMENT: Take an anonymous poll from your staff using a voting box where you ask them what your biggest weakness as a leader is. Tally up the votes and let your team know what the "winning" item was (this holds you accountable). Now Google how to fix this trait and start putting an action plan together to address it.

Staffs Judge on Every Decision You Make

"Example is not the main thing in influencing others. It is the only thing."
~Albert Schweitzer

"Nothing is so potent as the silent influence of a good example" ~James Kent

. . . . .

Right or wrong, when you are a leader, there are no "off days", there are no "half baked" decisions, and there is no "coasting" through the day. You are "up on stage" in front of your staff every moment of every day. It is what we signed up for, and it is what your boss believed you were capable of handling. Right or wrong we are in the spotlight setting the example for our team with every move we make.

When you look to enact change, to discipline a team member, or to rally the troops behind performance goals, what gets mentioned by those employees who are against what you are saying?

- The one time you didn't give a well thought out answer
- The one time you were dismissive
- The one decision you made incorrectly
- The one project you half-assed
- The one exception you made to the rule

It is these things that stick in your staff's minds as they observe you. And it is the elimination of these things that make everything you do as a leader easier. Great leaders don't have "off" days, or when they do, they are able to hide it and perform. Every decision is a test, a test that you are capable of passing with flying colors. Just take a breath, concentrate, and nail it. If you start hearing any of the above things you know you need to make a change.

One thing that can help mitigate these comments is open communication. Oftentimes it isn't even that you fell short when you were in the spotlight, it's that your actions were perceived wrong. Communicating the reason for your actions more regularly eliminates this and can even give you the benefit of the doubt.

LESSON ASSIGNMENT: Start a log of every time you hear one of the above five comments. Add to that every time you catch yourself doing something that could come back as one of those five comments. Track this for a few weeks and you may see a pattern in your behavior that you need to address.

Rethink Metrics

"Things don't change, only the way you look at them." ~Carlos Castaneda

"Just because something is easy to measure doesn't mean it's important." ~Seth Godin

· · · · ·

When was the last time you looked at the metrics you use every day? Have any of them changed in recent memory? Could there be better ones to use that reflect the changes in your business? Sometimes the answer is "No", the metrics you have are just fine, but sometimes there is new data you have access to, new business segments to measure, or just a more "enlightened" way of looking at things. Likewise, there may be data you were pulling for a special project long ago that is no longer needed.

While I am often preaching simplicity which usually means less data not more, or means streamlining existing operations, sometimes adding an extra ingredient makes all of the difference in the world, especially if metrics are a holdover from a different time or have not been flexible with growth.

The question to ask yourself honestly: Do they give you the insight you need?

- **What can be discarded** – First, see if there is any unnecessary work you are doing and noise you are being subjected to. These are distractions that are out of date and give little insight or actionable data. Alternatively, there may be reports that you can do less frequently like weekly, monthly or quarterly instead of as frequently as you do them now. Once these are cleared away, it gets easier to swallow doing a "new" report.
- **What can be enhanced** – Sales by hour instead of by day, add-on sales, more segmentation and granularity, the ability to drill down into the data. Are any of these worthwhile to get more insight and action? Or if that seems too cumbersome, perhaps you can do the "deep dive" of granular data on an as needed or less frequent basis.
- **What new data do we have access to** – Systems and databases evolve. Odds are that some of the "no, we can't access that data" requests you had in the past are no longer barriers. Likewise, sometimes new reports have been created in other departments. Go ask them.
- **With your ongoing experience/wisdom, is there a better metric that gives the insight you need** – As we grow in our careers we get better at determining what the triggers to performance are, sometimes these triggers are not being measured at all. Use what you know to discover better metrics.

While sales results and net income will always be valuable measures, there are plenty of data points that can be reviewed to see if they are worth the time to put on a report, and there may be better ways to measure performance that are just waiting to be put into action. Take a look, you may find that some changes could be beneficial.

LESSON ASSIGNMENT: What are your three most important metrics? There shouldn't be more than three or you aren't really prioritizing. Now tie all of your other metrics to those three. You want to focus and enhance those three as best you can, so this is where you look for more. If there are any that don't really tie to those three then you can look to cut them or do them more infrequently to make more time for the important metrics.

Should Do versus Need to Do

"It's never crowded along the extra mile" ~Wayne Dyer

"Good enough never is." ~Debbi Fields

• • • • •

When it comes to many of our duties and initiatives we often end up doing what we "need" to do to get whatever we are working on taken care of. This is balanced against what we "should" do to go the extra mile and ensure the product/service delights the customer. This often means that we have done only the bare minimum to get the job done.

- I need to eat, but I should eat better.
- I need to acknowledge Mother's Day to my wife, but I should take her out to dinner and get her flowers.

In the current competitive landscape, bare minimum thinking will eventually mean the decline and fall of your organization and department. Doing the "should" doesn't need to be a huge time consumer if you start tackling them early on in the process and stay on top of them throughout. Follow some of the guidelines below:

- **Prioritize the "shoulds"** – There are *a ton* of things you "could" do, but what we want is what you "should" do. Make a list and rank it by impact to the customer. Those near the bottom are now "coulds".
- **Tackle "shoulds" while tackling "needs"** – Manage your time and effort for maximum impact. Working concurrently on items means doing them while you are working on something else (most likely something complementary). This cuts down the time and effort investment by leveraging your focus.
- **Change project goals from "needs" to "shoulds"** – By changing the scope of your project up front you will be better equipped to make a plan to accomplish it.
- **Revisit the "shoulds"** – As the process moves along, opportunities will come up. Determine where they fit on the priority list (many things that come up are probably "coulds" and need to be prioritized as such). But don't limit your thinking and be sure to write it down, some of the best brainstorming takes place while working through problems.

Great companies and departments pack as much as possible into their efforts, in effect they get as many "shoulds" as possible into their output. Think of your work as you would think about a consumer electronic product. You generally buy the one with the most features. If you produce more features into you daily productivity, you will be more valuable and successful. Use the tips above to leverage your time for the most impactful "shoulds" and you will be well on your way.

LESSON ASSIGNMENT: Take your task list out and see if there are any that should be changed to include what "should" be done. Now prioritize a few of the "shoulds." Start with one this week, and plan on doing two next week. By planning you will make it easier and by doing one this week you will build momentum. Keep trying to increase the number of "shoulds" every week.

Don't Let a Detail Derail a Purpose

"Things which matter most must never be at the mercy of things which matter least." ~Johann Wolfgang von Goethe

"Don't throw the baby out with the bath water." ~Anonymous

. . . . .

Minding and managing details is essential to the proper functioning of your department and organization, of this there can be little debate. What I am speaking of in the title of this chapter is that all details are not created equal. The ability to separate the important details from the unimportant details is just as essential as paying attention to them in the first place. Many times in our focus on detail, we give them too much power and let them paralyze a project or distract us from more important things. Some of the more common areas this occurs in order of frequency:

- **Caught up in details that are irrelevant** – Don't let yourself get obsessed. Sometimes the thing we are focused on gains more importance than it should. Always prioritize the details so that you are handling the most impactful and are using your time in the best way. As Peter Drucker says "There is nothing so useless as doing efficiently that which should not be done at all."
- **Dismiss wisdom because it is surrounded by ignorance** – This is the "baby out with the bath water" scenario. There can be a terrible report, a worthless meeting, or a poorly thought out initiative, but that doesn't mean that there aren't areas where you can learn. Failure often brings about the best lessons, and while the fact remains that the overall point was missed, there is typically some usefulness there.
- **Detail as an excuse** – Finding any detail to excuse a missed timeline, unmet expectations, etc. regardless of whether it has anything to do with the issue. The classic example I see is, "Well they didn't do it either" which has no bearing on *your* deliverable.
- **Shooting the messenger** – We all have them in our companies, the people with the best intentions but who are relatively clueless. Many times we let this detail of their ability obscure that the point they are making has some worth. Listen intently and you may be able to mine a few nuggets of wisdom.

Details matter, but they are not everything. Think 80/20 rule where 80% of the benefit comes from 20% of the work. You must prioritize your perceptions for maximum effectiveness. While there is almost always a kernel of truth as to why it is actually important, that must be weighed like everything else, not just used as a veto.

LESSON ASSIGNMENT: Details often fall into two categories, quick and difficult. It is a real shame when we let a quick detail become a problem. Look to knock out the quick details right away when they pop up and clear away the noise surrounding the difficult details.

Fall in Love with Your Problems

"Management is the art of making problems so interesting that everyone wants to get to work and deal with them." ~Paul Hawken

"A problem is a chance for you to do your best." - Duke Ellington

. . . . .

Every business is based on solving a need/want of a consumer. Departments run no differently, and neither do careers. Successful companies, departments and people find a way to passionately pursue the problem they are solving. They define themselves by the problems they solve.

The first focus is The Problem.....then The Solution

You can't have great answers without great questions. As the quote says above, great managers help their staff get excited about solving the problems they face. If you can solicit interest in the problem, the solution you create will be that much better. Let me draw another parallel; whether it is Sudoku, Crossword Puzzles, or video games, the more challenging the problem, the more we will be drawn to it, and the more satisfied you will be when you solve it.

Your career, department and business should be about solving increasingly more difficult problems

So how do you get the motivation to strive for greater and greater problems, even in cases when you won't be rewarded for all of them?

- **Why is it important?** Tie it to something big. Don't be humble, make it seem as important and critical as possible. Your mind is like a muscle and you will get the most out of it when you test it with the most weight.
- **Give them ownership.** Your team can't be passionate if they don't feel they have a stake in it. Look for opportunities to get their ideas on how to solve the problem, then let them run with their idea. Alternatively, you can prevail to their sense of pride, whether it be personal, departmental, or company pride by making the success of the team their success. Eventual success against a great competitor is powerful motivation.
- **Free them from failure.** Most people's greatest fear is of failure. If you are going to free your team to be passionate about finding a solution, you need to assuage their concerns of failure.

The goal should be a self-perpetuating loop where you are seeking out bigger and bigger problems to solve as a department so that you can feel the rush of successfully meeting the challenge. The importance and size of the solution though, can only match the importance of the problem. Problem first, then solution.

LESSON ASSIGNMENT: Fear of failure is often what holds us back from taking on greater and greater challenges. Ask for anonymous ideas for what problems your area should take on next (maybe a submission box). Then pull your team together and vote on what to tackle next. This way you all share in the challenge and mitigate any individual failure.

Being Busy Makes Things Easier

"Bite off more than you can chew, then chew it. Plan more than you can do, then do it." ~Anonymous

"Determine never to be idle...It is wonderful how much may be done if we are always doing." ~Thomas Jefferson

. . . . .

One of the things that can make you more productive as a leader and as an employee is to strive to be in constant motion. I don't mean being busy for the sake of being busy, I mean putting a whole lot of the right kind of duties on your plate. When you have a lot to do, you are forced to work harder *and* smarter to get everything done, and working both hard and smart gets the *exact* sort of results we should look to achieve regularly.

- Have you ever noticed how focused you are when you are under a deadline?
- Have you ever noticed how you gain some perspective on what is a "little thing" and what is a "big thing" when you have no time for the little things?
- Have you ever noticed how problems get mowed over when you have the momentum of decision making on your side?

Why is it that these things take place? *Because you are hyper-focused on completion of a task/project* so that you can move on to the next thing. You don't have time to make mountains out of molehills, you multitask into every free minute you have (making phone calls while walking between meetings for instance), and you are forced to delegate tasks that can be delegated. There is something called the Parkinson Principle that states that any given task will grow to fill the time allotted to it. If you don't have time, you won't have your tasks expanding into useless time periods.

Now a few words of warning before your eyes get bigger than your stomach in regards to taking on work:

- No busy work – Make sure you are loading up on the right kind of work, not just doing things that your Supervisors or employees can do.
- Have back-up – You *will* occasionally take on too much, so you need a "go to" person for assistance on each project in case you are going to miss a deadline.
- Look for flexibility – You may find that priorities move around a lot, so try to maintain flexibility with the expectations you set for deadlines and be flexible yourself in what you may need to work on next.

But with that said, load up and watch your days fly by and your productivity soar. Being busy actually makes great results easier because you have the right kind of momentum throughout your day.

LESSON ASSIGNMENT: You can exercise sprinting even when you don't need to sprint. Create a task list of things to get done tomorrow that looks like what you might have on any typical day and see how many you can get done by *lunchtime* as opposed to throughout the day.

The Pathway to Leadership

"It is a mistake to look too far ahead. Only one link in the chain of destiny can be handled at a time." ~ Winston Churchill

"Only those who constantly retool themselves stand a chance of staying employed in the years ahead." ~Tom Peters

. . . . .

Career progression naturally lends itself to the correct leadership "path". You are a great employee, so you are promoted to lead. You are a great lead, so you are promoted to supervisor, then manager and higher. Along the way, you typically acquire a staff, and as you grow the number of staff members tends to as well. To put it succinctly:

- First you *Lead Yourself*
- Then you *Lead One*
- Then you *Lead a Team*
- Then you *Lead Many Teams*

But as with a familiar hiking trail where you will sometimes see new things you never saw before, so you should revisit your path to leadership to see if there is something new to discover. Is there a better way to lead yourself, your team and others? Those leaders who are constantly evaluating themselves and their techniques, and making adjustments based on that, are the ones who get ahead quickest.

- **Lead yourself** – You adjust with each role as the demands change. You adjust as the dynamic in your department/

organization changes. You adjust as you mature and discover what works and what doesn't.

- **Lead one** – Has your successor or sounding board changed or moved on? Once this person moves onward and upward do you have another protégé in mind? Is how you are leading them needing an evolution due to the ideas presented in the point above?
- **Lead a team** – Are you getting the results you anticipated? Is the team coming together as one unit? Are there new opportunities/dangers that have come along? Are you creating a structure that can "scale" to more teams?
- **Lead many teams** – Have you created metrics to help oversee the departments closely? Have those metrics changed? Are there new opportunities to build synergies between teams?

This circuitous evaluation utilizes your newly gained experience and wisdom to the fullest and ensures that no area of leadership goes untouched. The Pathway to Leadership is a long one, but has familiar milestones along the way. As you pass these milestones, reflect on what you have learned, what the present situation demands, and make the correct changes to your style and technique to fit the situation.

LESSON ASSIGNMENT: Schedule a meeting with yourself once a month to review these four areas of leadership and see what may have changed and where you can improve your leadership.

Quick Draws Aim Poorly

"If you don't have time to do it right, what makes you think you will have time to do it over?" ~Seth Godin

"It takes less time to do a thing right, than it does to explain why you did it wrong." ~Henry Longfellow

. . . . .

Short cuts and cutting corners will work out some of the time, but other times they will blow up in your face. I'm from Vegas, and I assure you the odds aren't worth the price. If you are going to put in the work, make sure it is something worthwhile. It is a terrible thing to go home at the end of the day and not be proud of what you have accomplished. Every bit of work that you do is a reflection on you and your abilities, make sure you are conveying the very best of yourself. Furthermore, you risk creating more work for yourself if the project doesn't reach its full potential, or worse, outright fails.

OK, so we all knew that already didn't we? But we all still fight the urge to cut corners. So why do we short change ourselves and our projects? Let's tackle the most common reason cited for taking the quick route to the end of our task:

Efficiency – We often think taking a short cut or cutting corners is the smart thing to do. While you may be looking to cut corners and save time and effort, you are often pushing the work to others, or pushing it off to yourself later. If you were to look at the total amount of work for the task (including what others do and the cost of redoing things), you'll usually find that spending the extra time to do it right to begin with comes out well ahead. Have you ever cleaned up the mess left by someone cutting corners? Probably. Did you think highly of the person who did it? Probably not. Think about that the next time you want to take the shortcut.

If you chronically take short cuts or cut corners, it will eventually catch up to you – either by reputation or horrendous mistake. What's worse is that you often cost yourself more time and effort. Make every instant the best example of your capabilities. Put another way, *make your work worth it*.

LESSON ASSIGNMENT: These things come up a lot at the end of the day. Instead of taking the shortcut to get out on time, either take the extra time and stay late to get it complete or push it to the next day (often there is no difference since nobody will look at it late at night). Then see what you think of the results versus what would have come out of your effort with the shortcut.

You Should Not Heed All Advice

"The worst vice is advice." ~Al Pacino – The Devil's Advocate

"Don't follow any advice, no matter how good, until you feel as deeply in your spirit as you think in your mind that the counsel is wise." ~David Seabury

· · · · ·

Step Up Before Your Employees Step Down

In an effort to brainstorm, get new ideas, get past the struggle, or just get unstuck, we are likely to try any number of things. One of those is to ask advice or to talk about the issue with others. But what do we do with that advice? Getting opinions is great, but sometimes those opinions come from questionable sources. You need to ensure you are taking advice from the right sources, so consider the following when looking to act on any advice:

- **Do they have relatable experience?** Have they walked a mile in shoes similar to yours? Have they dealt with this issue, or a similar issue, before?
- **What is their motivation?** Your peer may have competing ideas or an axe to grind with another department. Your boss might want you at work more. Your team may want you at work less. You just want to ensure that there are no ulterior motives.
- **How has their own advice worked for them?** It pays to look at where their decisions have led them. Are they successful? Are they fulfilled in work and life? If they aren't then consider their advice with a grain of salt.

Only when you have vetted the advice should you move forward. Not all advice is created equal: advice from my 4 year old on driving is usually not good advice (though telling me to slow down is sometimes correct). This method of review can be good when you have been given different advice from different people.

So just make sure that the advice you are given is weighted with some reality. Remember, just because someone gave you advice does not mean that you are not ultimately responsible for the results. After all, it was *you* that acted on the advice.

LESSON ASSIGNMENT: The next time you are thinking about getting advice on a topic, first write down three people who have been there before. It is these individuals you should seek out, not just the next person who comes through your office door.

Find a Mentor When Reaching for the Stars

"Good artists copy, great artists steal" ~Pablo Picasso

"By three methods we may learn wisdom: First, by reflection, which is noblest; Second, by imitation, which is easiest; and third by experience, which is the bitterest." ~Confucius

. . . . .

Whether you are stretching your management technique to learn how to operate at the next level of the career ladder or you have an incredibly ambitious project that you are spearheading, look for a mentor! Getting a coach who has been there before can speed up the process (which is *really* nice when you are looking for a promotion) and can offer a level of insurance as they have usually made a couple of the mistakes before. Finding a mentor is one of the most important things you can do for your success. So let's look at mentorship in each of these areas, then look at what to do when you can't find a mentor in your organization:

Career Mentors:

- **Look to your boss first** - They have the most vested interest in your performance and if they move up the ladder, that can mean an open spot for you to advance. Always remember that this is your role for your subordinates (be the boss you'd like to have). Unfortunately we don't always have a "mentor boss", it is for this reason I also look to the others listed below:
- **Lateral position to my boss (his/her peers)** – Oftentimes there is a superstar heading another area who enjoys sharing

ideas/wisdom. It is important that you are sensitive to their time as they have their own operation to oversee.
- **My boss's boss** - The third option is to go one step over your boss's head. You have the benefit of someone with a vested interest in your department's success, but there can be some friction with your boss as they may be concerned you are gunning for their job or jumping the chain of command. For this reason ensure that you discuss topics with your boss first, and ensure that you are not giving off *any* vibe that you are looking for your boss's job at the expense of their employment.
- **Break it up** – If you can't find the "perfect" mentor you can always look to specific traits in any of the above people that are mentor-worthy. This has worked very well for me in the past where I am able to "cherry pick" great traits from multiple people.

Project Mentors:

- **Anyone who has tackled this area before** – The obvious place to look are stakeholders in the area your project touches, or even those who have gone before you in this area or project. They can provide you with valuable advice on what has worked in the past, or where trouble spots lie.
- **Anyone who has tackled *some sort of big project*** – Your only other option is someone who has tackled some sort of project before. At least in this case you are getting some general advice. Many things like lack of resources or time are common issues across any project.

This is all well and good, but more often than we would care to admit, we can't find a mentor in our organization. Sometimes there is one, but they do not have the time, or it would be a political hot potato to work with them. When this happens, we have a few options:

- **Head to the web** – This page or the thousands like it. Even a Google search on the specific topic can yield good resources (news articles, question boards, etc)
- **Head to your network** – Maybe a friend or colleague can offer some advice, or ask for some advice from their network.
- **Head out the door** – Perhaps if there is no one "mentor worthy" in your organization, you may be in the wrong organization. Just a thought.

So look for advice and assistance whenever you can. The learning curve in your career and projects is often long and steep. Anything you can do to speed along that curve will benefit you.

LESSON ASSIGNMENT: Make a list of your possible mentors and what they are particularly great at. Now see if you can schedule weekly one-on-one sessions with them to go over your tasks and performance. If this is your boss, this should be no issue, if it isn't then you may need to space it out to once every two weeks or once a month. A mentor-worthy individual will appreciate you taking the initiative.

Your Business and Career Runs on Promises

"The older I get the less I listen to what people say and the more I look at what they do." ~Andrew Carnegie

"It's an immutable law in business that words are words, explanations are explanations, promises are promises but only performance is reality" ~Unknown

Step Up Before Your Employees Step Down

. . . . .

Do what you say you are going to do and fulfill your obligations. That is the expectation of a great leader. This shouldn't be news to any of us, but it is sometimes *very* difficult to maintain given that we are all pulled in several directions and there are many factors out of our control. But if we don't fulfill our promises to our employer and our customers, then we risk losing both. So what are some things to keep in mind that will help us fulfill our promises:

- **Set reasonable expectations** – One of the first places people fail is overpromising. Your promises are really just expectations phrased differently. It is a big temptation because it makes the conversation easier, but instead try for "reasonable" expectations and you'll find much less tension. In the case of your job description having an unreasonable expectation, I recommend prioritizing with your boss and delegating where possible. Regardless, it needs to be addressed lest they feel you are not performing. And PS: Don't set up an unrealistic job description for subordinates, it's just not nice.
- **Expect the unexpected** – Stuff happens, there's no way around it. So given this fact, you must always "pad" timelines and workloads for the inevitable surprises. If you do this one thing in your work day, a lot of things will fall into place. I personally put a lot of tasks on my calendar and I rarely allot less than 15 minutes to them which automatically creates buffer space for unexpected things that pop-up.
- **Always stay on top of your game** – If you start falling behind, it will snowball. That's why it is important to take care of as many of your tasks as possible, as soon as possible. This will result in more "peaks and valleys" in your workflow where some days are packed and are 10-12 hours long and some are lighter and only 8 hours long so take and enjoy the breaks when you can. If you don't keep on top of it, emergencies will cause conflicts.

So just keep this in mind: Your ability to do what you say and when you say you'll do it is absolutely vital to your relationships and your career. Keep the three things above in mind and you'll be able to control things much better.

LESSON ASSIGNMENT: Setting reasonable expectations is one of the toughest things to do because we want to expect the best from ourselves and everyone around us. For this reason it is important to practice this initial step. For the next week, push back your promised timeframes. If you want to say one hour, say two hours. If you want to say one day, say two days. Tomorrow instead of today, afternoon instead of morning, etc. Yes, you may get some push back and in those cases it is OK to make an adjustment since you have padded others. Do this for a week and see what the effect is on the success of your promises and on your stress level.

One Battle at a Time

"The journey of a thousand miles begins with a single step" ~Lao Tsu

"It is a mistake to look too far ahead. Only one link in the chain of destiny can be handled at a time." ~ *Winston Churchill*

. . . . .

With all of the duties we have in management and all of the directions we are pulled, it is common for us to be spread too thin and to lose focus. This typically results in us working on everything at the same time to some degree, getting very few things across the finish line, slowing down processes, feeling overwhelmed, and a host of other issues. This is why focus is so key to our day in day out management.

Three areas I have seen this most recently in my own work:

- **Poorly Performing Area** – Usually there is not one root cause to poor performance, there are unfortunately several. It is very easy to spend your time listing out all of the problems and beginning work on all of them at the same time. It feels good to see we've been entrusted to a large task, and it looks good to be addressing more than we can possibly handle. Unfortunately, if your focus is everywhere, by definition you have no focus. *Make your list a checklist.* Tackle one of the causes, fix it, lock in the success, and move on to the next on. It is in this way you make step by step progress.
- **Need to Reestablish Positive Momentum** – A great winning streak always starts with a single win. Inevitably in business you'll run across those patches where your best efforts just don't produce positive results. During those times it is correct to focus on the end goal that comes from a number of successes to fix the destination in your mind, but you need to lock in that first success. So focus on the next success, not the entire string. To use another sports metaphor, take it one game at a time.
- **Your Day to Day Tasks** – Oftentimes we walk in the door of the office and our "To do list" is already hopelessly long. Instead of getting demoralized, talking about how much there is to do, or even avoiding the tasks, just get to work!!! See how fast you can get the first task done. Get one task out of the way, then get another, then another. Before you know it, half the list is gone.

You don't always need to survey the entire battlefield of your day. Many times it is better to focus on one thing at a time, break large tasks in to smaller pieces, and methodically tackle your work. By doing so, you may find that you accomplish more for the same amount of work.

LESSON ASSIGNMENT: Take the biggest task you have on your calendar and break it up into its component parts. Create a checklist from those components and start checking them off.

What is Your Mission or Basic Values

"When your values are clear to you, making decisions becomes easier." ~Roy E. Disney

"There are so many men who can figure costs, and so few who can measure values." ~Unknown

. . . . .

Do you have a "True North" guideline that you can use to guide all of your business decisions? My guess is that you either have one that is so unused that nobody can remember what it was, or just as likely, you don't have one at all. These are typically known as Mission Statements or Core Values in most organizations. Some of the more common are:

- Do what is best for the customer
- Maximize shareholder value
- Innovate and create groundbreaking products

These are the statements that clarify almost any situation in the business to guide the decision. If you don't have one, or don't know of one, then we can start from scratch. Even if your organization has one, that doesn't mean that you can't create one for your department (and in fact, it is usually helpful to do so). If you want to create a mission statement, ask yourself a few questions to direct your thought:

- **How do you differ?** – Sometimes, but not always, it is helpful to look at how you differ from the competition. What makes you special? That way you can keep focused on staying that way.
- **How are you going to accomplish everything?** – Are there key things that you need to do to be successful? Key things to keep in mind? Pick the most central and consider including it.
- **Why are you in business?** – What is your purpose? When it comes right down to it, what do you do? And how do you do it exceptionally well?
- **Who are your customers?** - Who do you serve? The world? The luxury market? Expectant mothers? The automotive industry? - If this is for your department specifically, the answer may be different between different areas.
- **What perceptions do you want to convey?** - Do you want to be the most affordable? Most efficient? Most timely? Most luxurious? Try to be more specific than just "best".

You want your Mission Statement to be *concise*, which is one of the keys to making it useful in focusing your actions. The best are very short, usually not more than one sentence. It is also useful once you come up with a few ideas on your own, to involve stakeholders in your area to get their thoughts and refine it even further.

Knowing what you value and what your purpose is can make the decision making process significantly easier, which frees up more time for other things!

LESSON ASSIGNMENT: I think you can anticipate what I am going to say....make a Mission Statement. Go through all of the above questions and come up with a definition of your purpose. Maybe it doesn't need to be as concise as one sentence to start with, but get something in place to define who you are and your purpose.

What Can YOU Work On

"You get the best out of others when you get the best out of yourself." ~Harvey S. Firestone

"By stretching yourself beyond your perceived level of confidence you accelerate your development of competence." ~Michael Gelb

· · · · ·

We focus outward a lot. What can our staff improve on? What can our boss improve on? What can our peers work on? But don't forget that there are things that *we* need to work on ourselves. Our management style, our skillsets, our project planning capabilities are all things that we need to be continuously improving on. Oftentimes our focus stays on the outside on what others do and we neglect ourselves and our own improvement.

Leadership is about getting work done through others, but that does not mean that we shouldn't be focused on ourselves from time to time. So for those who don't have a plan for self-improvement yet, here's a simple one:

- **List what you would like to work upon** – Giving better feedback, managing e-mail better, Excel, etc.
- **Set a plan to work on the items** – Are there blogs, books, or courses to take that can assist? Once you have the resources available you can come up with a plan and timeline.
- **Work the plan** – Just do it, nothing more to say

- **Rinse and repeat** – Now that time has gone by, priorities and needs may have changed. It's good to reassess your list before starting the next trait.

There are always things that we can work on and things we *should* work on. Don't spend so much time working through others that you don't leave time to work on your own improvement. That improvement on yourself will help you work through others even better.

LESSON ASSIGNMENT: What are your three biggest weaknesses? Now take the easiest one on the list (let's build some momentum before tackling the final one) and put together a plan to work on it.

What Got You Here, Won't Get You There

"Progress is impossible without change and those who cannot change their minds cannot change anything." ~George B. Shaw

"Success is less a function of grandiose predictions than it is a result of being able to respond rapidly to changes as they occur." ~Jack Welch

. . . . .

What got us to where we are will not necessarily make us successful in our new position, and oftentimes must be discarded. This was brought to my attention while I was sitting in a meeting with my boss and he was talking about how he wanted a particular situation handled. What he recommended would have been the *exact* opposite approach he would have (and probably did) use when he was in the position of the manager he was speaking to. Was this a little disingenuous of him? Not really. In his new position he had a new perspective that afforded him a different insight into the situation.

As you move up the Corporate Ladder your vision needs to widen. The success of a leader depends entirely on how they lead their people, and the productivity that their leadership enables. With each new change in position, you should reflect on the skills you have used to get there, the skills you have that may have gone unused, and the skills you need to be successful. If you don't make this assessment you risk maintaining habits that while successful before, are now detrimental.

- **Skills that got you to where you are:** What skills are less important now than they were in your prior position? Which skills are even more important?
- **Skills that went unused in your prior position:** Do you have any skills that you can now use that you couldn't/didn't before?
- **Skills you need to be successful:** What new skills will you need to acquire to be successful? How can you get them and/or who can you mentor under?

Perspective changes as you ascend the ranks of your business. Ensure that your skillset and behavior reflects this new perspective and you will set yourself up for the next rung on the ladder.

LESSON ASSIGNMENT: What skills do you need right now to be successful in your current position? Make a list of these and choose one to begin acquiring this week.

Repair Relationships

"A cardinal principle of Total Quality escapes too many managers: you cannot continuously improve interdependent systems and processes until you progressively perfect interdependent, interpersonal relationships." ~Stephen Covey

"All lasting business is built on friendship." ~Alfred A. Montapert

· · · · ·

Your relationships are one of the most fundamental tools you have to get things done. Your relationships with employees, suppliers, your peers, your boss, and customers can set you up for success, or can doom you to failure.

In the course of business it is natural for some of these relationships to grow strained from time to time. It is important that we look to repair these as soon as possible, but the first step is to recognize that there is an issue to begin with. To that end, start with these questions:

- **Who are they?** Is there anyone you know who has an issue with you? Have you let anyone down or come up short on a deliverable recently? Have you needed to make decisions that were unpopular with one of these parties? Any of these could, or could not, lead to a relationship strain.
- **What happened?** Was there a legitimate reason, were you in the wrong, or was it simply a misunderstanding? Is it personality related? Is it product related? Be sure to think about it objectively, because if you don't address the actual problem, it could just get worse.

- **How can you fix it?** Do you need to adjust your approach? Do you need to talk through the "why" of what occurred? Do you need to apologize? Remember to do what is right for the organization/department, this always leads to success in the end. Sometimes that means being the "bigger person".
- **How soon can you fix it?** Now try to fix it even sooner. Repairing the relationship and moving on helps everyone be more productive.

Often we let problems fester instead of taking the necessary action to nip it in the bud. Nothing is worse than having an issue pop up that requires the collaboration of one of these strained relationships. It is when that happens that you'll wish you had done what you could to repair that relationship when you had the chance.

LESSON ASSIGNMENT: List three people or groups of people that you have a strained relationship with and endeavor to take one action this week to address the strain. Then two actions next week and three actions the week after next. By then it should be time to make a new list and start over. It is a good idea to do this once a month to ensure that no ill will is allowed to take root.

Rearrange Your Day for Maximum Effectiveness

"Anticipate the difficult by managing the easy." ~Lao Tsu

"Time is the scarcest resource and unless it is managed nothing else can be managed." ~Peter Drucker

Step Up Before Your Employees Step Down

. . . . .

A few of us are just naturally energetic and hyper-focused all day long, but for many of us (me included) there are times in the day where we are a little "out of it". I've heard it said before that we have a limited number of good decisions in the day so we need to manage them wisely, and while I'm not sure that's the case, I think that what the line was getting at is that we simply aren't at our best every single moment of the day. The energy product 5 Hour Energy identified it as that "2:30 feeling". As with many things, this is not a problem in and of itself, *if* we identify it and do something about it. Remember the importance of managing ourselves just as much as we manage our staff. To help with this aspect I recommend the following questions, then we'll get into what to do with that info:

- **First: What time of day are you at your best and worst?** For me, I am at my best throughout the morning, and my worst right after lunch and getting better as it gets closer to heading home.
- **Second: Are there tasks that energize you?** Everyone has those tasks they enjoy that either give a jolt of satisfaction at a job well done or inspire you to reach to the next level (for me it is customer meetings and performance statistics).
- **Third: Beware the landmines!** And there are some tasks that we just dread doing. Make sure to identify those as well.

Once we have identified the timeframes and activities that affect our energy level we can take steps with the flexible tasks we have in our day to minimize both the impact of our downtime and the total amount of it:

- **Leverage the lulls** – This is where I place routine tasks that do not require a huge amount of thought. Under no circumstances do I place a landmine in the middle of a lull, it

saps energy and productivity and can seemingly last forever. In my case I try to do simple things after lunch.
- **Attack the lulls** – Right after the routine task, I make every attempt to do one of my energizing tasks to pull me out of the lull as quickly as possible. After an energizing task is an appropriate place to put a landmine. So I will set up a customer meeting/call or pull together some metrics.
- **Leverage the best parts of your day** – Mix in some landmines in the middle of some energetic tasks to knock them out while maintaining momentum. I tackle my toughest tasks at the beginning of my day after building up a bit of momentum with simple tasks.
- **Attack the best parts of your day** - This is where you should do all of your strategic thinking and big decision making if at all possible. Ride this wave as far as you can by being careful not to put a landmine at the end which will kill the momentum. Take care of these landmines well ahead of time. Depending on when your lulls are you can look to shorten them by stretching your best parts of the day.

Plan your day for effective action. Maximize your energetic times by doing your most important work during these time and extending the momentum as much as possible. Minimize your lulls by doing routine tasks during this time and use your energetic tasks to pull yourself out as quickly as possible.

LESSON ASSIGNMENT: I think the step by step was laid out pretty well above so get to it. Know that you will be constantly learning, so be prepared to refine it for maximum effect.

Your Job is to Deal with the Non-Ideal Situations

"Do not bring me your successes; they weaken me. Bring me your problems; they strengthen me." ~Anonymous

"The measure of success isn't if you have a tough problem, but whether it's the same one you had last year." ~J.F. Dulles

. . . . .

As a leader, your role is to chart the course for the department and/or see that it is following the course that has been set. Listen, if it was easy, everyone would do it. Put another way, almost any monkey could run the department with the ideal tools, staff, and support. You are there to deal with the problems as they come up, that's your "real world" role. I see too many Leaders "wigging out" every time there is a problem or a lack of ideal resources like they can't believe they are being inconvenienced by it.

You took the job for the challenge and to have the responsibility and ownership, you were given the job because you were deemed to be up to the task. The task of dealing with the non-ideal situations, process failures, the lack of resources, and all other problems is what comes with the territory. But with that said, there are a few things to keep in mind to minimize the issues and deal with them when they come up in the best way possible:

- **Get ahead of it** – The best way to handle a problem is before it even becomes a problem. What are your most common issues or resource shortfalls? What is the cause of those issues? What can

you do to handle the cause, or at least get a notification so you are ready for the problem?
- **Push the responsibility down** – How many times has your staff just handed over the problem to you when they could have tackled it themselves? Look to your empowerment options for your staff. Encourage them to take ownership and make the decision. Coach them when they pass something off you feel they could have handled and you will minimize the number of times they need to come to you.
- **By setting the attitude example** – You have the ability to defuse much of the stress and anxiety that comes with these issues just by displaying the right way of handling it. Take the opportunity to "model the way" for your staff.
- **Plan for problems** – They are going to happen, so include some time for them in your project and include some time for them in your day (If your calendar is filled with back-to-back tasks, you're begging for trouble). Put another way, if you aren't ahead of schedule you are begging to find yourself behind schedule.
- **Deal as it comes** – The least welcome option is dealing with it as it comes up, but you need to, so just do it with as much grace as you can.
- **Fix it when it's over** – Don't forget to try to prevent the problem from occurring again. Whether it is coaching the employee, following up with another department, instituting a new process, or any other of the myriad of ways there are to prevent issues from occurring, just be sure to do them. You may not have been able to get ahead of it this time, but you can get ahead of it the next time.

I wish we didn't have as many problems to deal with as we do, but the simple fact is that we need to be ready for them because they are the reason we have the position we have. Great leaders do more with less, and work towards the "ideal" by proving themselves capable of producing results.

LESSON ASSIGNMENT: I think the key to all of this is in having the right attitude. Focus this week on dealing with problems as if you expected them to occur (which shouldn't be too far off since we know they will come) and simply handle them like you would a regular task with constructive and positive actions. Odds are you will struggle with this initially, but fortunately you will have plenty of opportunities to practice. See how I made that a positive?

Be the Change You Want To See

"A leader leads by example not by force." ~Sun Tzu

"I cannot trust a man to control others who cannot control himself." ~ Robert E. Lee

"Example is not the main thing in influencing others. It is the only thing." ~Albert Schweitzer

. . . . .

What do you do when the "Boss" is the biggest breaker of rules and policies? Are you more apt to follow the letter of the law at all times or bend the rules occasionally? One of the easiest ways to create dysfunction in your department is to live by a different set of rules than the people you oversee. If you want an organization with integrity you need to be consistent with what you say *and* what you do. When you break your own rules, regardless of the logic, you:

- **Undermine the authority of your policies** – Your staff may ask whether it is really that important if you are willing to break the rule or policy.
- **Encourage resentment** – Often rules, policies and guardrails are looked upon as something that holds people back from fulfilling their duties, if you are breaking those policies, then you are viewed as taking the easy road.
- **Create an environment of confusion and lack of control** – Instead of knowing what you are going to do, or being sure of what it is they should do, your staff is left guessing. Never a good thing to foster.

We see this a lot in customer interactions where the leader steps in to an issue that was brought to their attention and proceeds to break procedure to make it easier on themselves and "solve" the problem for the customer. It is not always easy, but by following your own policies and rules, you set the example and make it as clear and easy as possible to follow them. How much more powerful is it when you say, "well even I do not deviate from that rule?" You set the example, you set the tone for your department and the result is in the buy-in that you see, don't forget it.

LESSON ASSIGNMENT: List out the rules that you break and the extra empowerment you give yourself. This might take a while just because you don't think of it in those terms (not because the list is crazy long). Now see which of these rules truly need to be in place and what empowerment you can give your team that you already give yourself.

Don't Tell Me, Show Me Instead

"Determine never to be idle...It is wonderful how much may be done if we are always doing." ~Thomas Jefferson

"The difficult can be done immediately, the impossible takes a little longer." ~Army Corp of Engineers

. . . . .

One of the biggest differentiators between "Good" leaders and "Great" leaders is that a good leader will tell you what they are going to do (they have a plan), a *great* leader tells you what they have *already done* (their plan is already in action). I think about this fact when I am preparing for a weekly or monthly update meeting with my boss. A good boss will not ask you to tell them, they will ask you to show them.

A focus on action can be one of the best things for you to develop in your career and one of the best traits for your team to adopt. It keeps the momentum moving forward and eliminates the dead spaces in the day and any thought of "paralysis by analysis". Some tricks of the trade that I have learned.

- **Get things in motion as soon as possible** – Once a task has been assigned, get the ball rolling. As soon as you're out of the meeting or read the e-mail, get to stepping. Ask yourself how much you can get done in that first 30 minutes.

- **Identify the most important things** – What does the boss care about most, no amount of other work will matter if the main points aren't addressed
- **Clear the hour before the next meeting** – This allows you to check progress and "button up" any loose ends you have, and possibly get moving on even more next steps so that you have made as much progress as possible.

The key is to be action focused, not talking focused. If achievement takes time, it is best to get started right away!

LESSON ASSIGNMENT: What 10 things on your "To-do List" haven't been started, or if there isn't enough of those, which ones have you not acted on today. What action step can you take *right now* to get going again?

Relax When Looking at the Huge Work in Front of You

"A clear vision, backed by definite plans, gives you a tremendous feeling of confidence and personal power." ~Brian Tracy

"Nothing is particularly hard if you divide it into small jobs." ~Henry Ford

· · · · ·

Do you ever get frustrated and/or paralyzed when looking at the enormity of the task, or the enormity of the amount of work that you need to get done? I'd be willing to bet that most of us have at some point. What tends to happen when we give in to this feeling of enormity? We get stressed, and:

- We work too fast – which often leaves the work incomplete.
- We split our focus between multiple tasks – which often leaves our work inaccurate.
- We set a frantic tone in the department – which leaves everyone else on edge.
- We don't do anything – "OMG, OMG, I don't believe how much work I need to get done. I need to do this, then this, then the other thing." All the while we aren't actually doing anything.

"So that's great" you say, "but what am I supposed to do about it!!!" There are a few things I recommend when the enormity of your job starts staring you straight in the face:

- **Start working on a task right away** – Taking action is empowering. One thing I have found is that oftentimes what I consider a huge task isn't nearly as bad as I think. With some swift action it can be halfway complete or entirely complete in short order.
- **Break it out into steps** – You need and want a plan. This takes the murky future and puts some clarity to it. Making the unknown a "known" puts you at ease and focuses your work.
- **Lean on your past success** – Be confident in the knowledge you have been through this before and made it through just fine.

Stress rarely leads to our best work and has a long term negative effect on not only our performance, but the performance of those we supervise as well. So relax and enjoy the challenge, you're up for it!

LESSON ASSIGNMENT: Let's focus on the last of the three actions above. Make a list of the big problems you have successfully brought across the finish line. Now put that list next to your monitor. The next time you start feeling overwhelmed, or in need of a "pick me up", then reference this list of successes to show how much you can accomplish.

See What You Need to on an Excel Spreadsheet

"You can see a lot by looking" ~Yogi Berra

"It's not what you look at that matters, it's what you see." ~Henry David Thoreau

. . . . .

Once you learn Excel, you'll quickly get tasked with doing more and more in it. As your talent grows you learn what to highlight for the audience and what to de-emphasize that can be used for reference if there are questions. While this serves the purpose of "telling the story" of the information, when you receive spreadsheets from others you want to make sure you are seeing what you are supposed to see and are guarding yourself from those who take a more malicious tack and look to flat out hide negative information in the numbers to make themselves look better.

Excel is a wonderful tool, but at its more advanced levels it becomes an art form, and art sometimes requires interpretation. There is a lot of information, a lot going on, and a myriad of ways to present the data. So how do you make sure it is painting the picture it is supposed to and not *just* what the other person wanted to convey?

- **Don't take it at face value** – Get clear on what you are looking for. The number at the right or at the bottom may not be the one you really want to look at. (or for that matter numbers that are formatted like they are important). Sometimes you might want to see sales, cost, net income, etc.
- **Look for flaws of logic** – Work through the process yourself, does it make sense on the page.
- **Wade through the sea of data** – If it is an enormous spreadsheet, start compartmentalizing the data and/or start at the beginning (or even the end in some cases). Look for what is important and "set aside in your mind" what isn't important. Most of the data on large spreadsheets is there to do a "deep dive" if the important number warrants looking into.
  - **Look for hidden information** – One of the most common tactics of the more unscrupulous is to hide bad numbers in a sea of data. When I am presented with an overly complicated spreadsheet I am immediately on guard for this.
- **Ask what you expected to see** – Does it make sense? Does it convey the information you expected? Basically, does it pass the smell test. If it doesn't then look deeper.
- **Don't be afraid to ask for changes** – Do you want to see a chart or something else to highlight the data? Trends are usually more apparent in charts than in raw numbers. Make sure you have the context you need and make sure you are clear on what changes you want implemented so there isn't an unending stream of changes.

I used to despise Excel, but as I became more familiar with it I learned that it was one of the most powerful tools out there. With that said it takes experience to be able to look at a spreadsheet and extract the information that helps you manage the business better. So use some of the hints above, and practice, practice, practice.

LESSON ASSIGNMENT: The key to understanding is to walk step by step through the spreadsheet and ask questions as you go. As you get more practice over the next month you will find more and more flaws and your team will begin learning how you want information presented.

Work with What You Have, Don't Wait For "Pie in the Sky"

"Make the workmanship surpass the materials." ~Ovid

"Don't measure yourself by what you have accomplished, but by what you should have accomplished with your ability." ~John Wooden

. . . . .

We all want to have more/better resources to work with:

- "Well if I only had better equipment…."
- "If I only had the time to train more…."
- "Whenever our budget increases…."
- "Once the enhancements are in place we'll go live…."

Rarely in your business career will you have the perfect situation from an equipment, resource, time and money perspective. If that were the case, about half of all managers would be out of a job. We get paid to make the most out of what we have, and most businesses find it is easier and cheaper to employ more managers than to spend the money on all of the other things (and they are not necessarily wrong, believe it or not). So given that our job description can be summarized with the phrase "Make more with less", I have the following suggestions for dealing with the reality:

- **Get perfection out of your mind and get to the starting place** – Something is better than nothing, waiting is not an option, so start somewhere. Babies crawl before they can walk because they want to get somewhere, similarly you can learn skills along the way.
- **Prioritize, prioritize, prioritize** – The 80/20 rule says that 80% of the benefit comes from 20% of the input. You can't have it all, so stick with what you want most.
- **Anticipate, anticipate, anticipate** – Since you don't have the luxury of mistakes, unintended consequences, dealing with emergencies, etc. one of your priorities (from above) needs to be to anticipate changes. If you get out ahead of changes to your department you can better utilize the resources you have to react to it.

Making the best of what they have is what every great leader should do with ease, and it is paramount to your success. So don't use the excuses above and fixate on what you don't have, odds are you have plenty to make a great run at your goals. Get to it!

LESSON ASSIGNMENT: What have you been waiting on? A project, a new initiative, the next step in something? How can you get started today with what you have available to you?

Do You Have The Right People on Your Team?

"Effective leaders help others to understand the necessity of change and to accept a common vision of the desired outcome." ~John Kotter

"As a leader, you're probably not doing a good job unless your employees can do a good impression of you when you're not around." ~Patrick Lencioni

. . . . .

As you navigate the many changes that will be thrust upon you, it is important that you ensure you have the right people in your corner. Your team typically has as much influence on each other as you have on them, so it is important that you make sure you have the right people on your side. When rolling out initiatives, training and projects, being able to have control over "the narrative" is essential to quick adoption. Not all employees are created equal both in performance and their ability to bring out the best in each other. So who are the team members that are influencing their peers?

- **The high performers** – Recognized and unrecognized for their exceptional performance. These are the people others admire, even if they don't admit it to themselves.
- **The "social" elite** – The ones everyone likes, the ones that are tied in to the gossip, and above all the ones who talk the most (ten silent allies are trumped by one talker who isn't on your side).
- **The new blood** – Newly hired employees are the reinforcements that add new vigor to one side of an argument/opinion or the other.

It seems somewhat contrived to seek out "allies" among your workforce, but when you think about it, shouldn't you be trying to make all of your employees your allies in business and business decisions? So why not start with the ones who give you the most impact? The reality though, is that people are complex, and even though your staff is on your team, all of them are probably not "on your team" with every decision you make for whatever personal reasons.

So when rolling things out to your team, the best way to ensure that you are controlling the narrative is to be as clear as possible as to *why* you are doing what you are doing. Secondarily to that, is to reach out to the influencers on your staff and make sure they understand. That way when the inevitable talk takes place around the water cooler, you will have relayed your message to the right people.

LESSON ASSIGNMENT: Write down the members of your team that fall into the above three groups, then pick one of the groups to spend a little more time with this week and see if they are "on your team". If they aren't then you know where you need to spend some time and effort getting your points across.

Keep Checking Your Map

"There is nothing so useless as doing efficiently that which should not be done at all." ~Peter Drucker

"Learn how to separate the majors and the minors. A lot of people don't do well simply because they major in minor things." ~Jim Rohn

. . . . .

Sometimes we are so focused on improving our operation that we lose perspective of the overall picture. It is essential that our actions are always aligned with the overall goals of the organization. If you don't know what your destination is, you may be working hard and productively, but not necessarily on what you should be. Or worse yet, you could be going in the wrong direction and completely wasting your time. So what good things do we try to do that may not be keeping the end in mind:

- **Focus on small things, not big things** – Example: focusing on greeting customers as they walk in, but not being available to answer questions once they get into the product aisles.
- **Focus on improving the wrong things** – Example: ensuring the display cases are dusted daily, but not focused on whether you have enough inventory of the best sellers or whether your staff has the product knowledge to sell what is in the cases.
- **Working with your "nose to the grindstone"** – Example: working with your head down, just focused on getting through the pile of work in front of you without looking around at certain times to see whether the time could be better spent

elsewhere. The highest priority an hour ago may not be a high priority now.

As you can see, the end goal isn't always the only thing needed, priorities are as well. The way to get both is to lay out a plan to get to the goal. The more detailed the plan, the less likely you are to stray from the goal, get lost in lower priorities, or inexplicably stop on one step. A few things to get you started:

- **Clearly define the goal** – What it looks like, what numbers should be reached, and what is the benefit.
- **What milestones can you hit along the way** - Short term, intermediate, and milestones between milestones. You need to be able to assess progress to determine if you need to change directions.
- **What resources do you have** - People, processes, overhead, product, training, etc. These are the tools and materials that you have to work with to reach the milestones and goals above.

The idea is that you have a goal and you not only build the map to get there, but just like any journey, you are constantly looking at the map to make sure you are heading in the right direction towards the eventual goal.

LESSON ASSIGNMENT: Get in alignment with your goals. What are the three most important objectives of the organization? Now take a look at your "to-do" list for today and see how many of those directly relate to the main three objectives. It is these tasks that you should prioritize first in your day.

Why I Hate PowerPoint and What to Learn From It

"However beautiful the strategy, you should occasionally look at the results."
~Winston Churchill

"Tell me and I forget. Teach me and I remember. Involve me and I learn."
~Benjamin Franklin

. . . . . .

Probably the most consistently misused tool across all industries is PowerPoint. It is meant to enhance presentations, however, it now has a tendency to diminish the impact of a presentation. Just ask yourself if it would be easier to stay focused (or awake even) during the last presentation you attended if they didn't use anything on the projector and just talked?

What's even worse is that there is an enormous amount of time spent reformatting information into a PowerPoint presentation that has already been gathered, and often presented, in another program (Word and Excel being the most obvious). It *is* important to "sell" things by presenting them well, but if you aren't selling something to an outside entity, or at least persuading people, then don't waste the time. So what are the specific problems with how PowerPoint is used?

- **Focused on the screen not you** – PowerPoint should be the window dressing to your presentation. The best communication style is where they can see you and hear your voice, which is what establishes a strong connection between you and your

audience. If people spend more than 50% of their time looking at the screen instead of you, you're doing it wrong.
- **Duplicate work wastes time** – How many times have you created a great spreadsheet that is very presentable, then have to spend 20-30 minutes reformatting it to look good on a PowerPoint slide? You actually need to do the same thing with most of your content in PowerPoint. It is rarely the original format. As mentioned above, unless you *really* need to sell you opinion/project you have to ask whether your time could more productively be spent elsewhere.
- **People don't know how to use it.**
  - They read it – It is not supposed to include every word you say, it is supposed to highlight information or add value to what you say.
  - Use boring slides – If your information is important enough to display on the big screen you might want to add a graph, or at least a nice background. Just putting numbers up on the screen is uninteresting and mitigates the impact of the numbers.
  - Try too hard to energize it – The opposite of the above. The information gets obscured by sound effects, animation, and cluttered screens.

So what should you do?

- **Don't read off the screen** – Your audience can read, so don't bother. Better yet, try including only pictures, graphs, and charts in your next presentation to force yourself to differentiate the content.
- **Don't pass out copies** – You want your audience focused on you. If you give them more choices of where to spend their attention (the screen, the handout, or you) you have just increased the opportunities for them to choose an option you don't really want them to choose.
- **Don't duplicate content** – The one thing I would recommend passing out is any content (like spreadsheets) that you have

already created, then reference the handout on the presentation slide. This saves you the times of recreating the wheel.
- **Use templates** – There are tens of thousands of free templates online that will dress your presentation up, capture attention, but not look too gaudy. This saves you the time of trying to come up with something original and pretty.

PowerPoint is a fantastic tool, but just as you wouldn't want to use a wrench as a hammer, it needs to be used in the right way. If used correctly, you will find your next presentation is far livelier and successful.

LESSON ASSIGNMENT: The next PowerPoint presentation you need to do, try to include no text whatsoever. The next one after that you can include text, but any numbers must be included in a graph or chart. Once you are comfortable with those two (I don't want you spending too much time on the learning curve at any one time) try integrating both concepts.

The Fish Stinks From the Head

"Always bear in mind that your own resolution to succeed is more important than any one thing." - Abraham Lincoln

"Hold yourself responsible for a higher standard than anybody expects of you. Never excuse yourself." ~Henry Ward Beecher

. . . . .

Step Up Before Your Employees Step Down

The title of this chapter comes from an old saying related to accountability. If your department (or you for that matter) isn't successful, you need only look in the mirror to place blame. It is *your* team, *your* career, *your* department, and *your* immediate responsibility to see that it is successful. Now yes, there are many times it is your boss, or their boss, or the company culture that has created a framework for dysfunction, but even with that, you can reach for success in areas you control. And you control a lot, so try:

- **Owning it** – One of the biggest mistakes a leader makes is throwing up his/her hands and believing that they do not have any control over the success of the department. Giving up your ownership leaves you completely incapable as a leader. But the fact is that you control a lot of things and paramount among them is how you react to all of the negative things in a corporate environment and how they are rolled out. Focus on owning the situation, don't look for the first opportunity to discount it when things get tough. It is your responsibility to flexibly deal with the management of your department, so *own it*.
- **Look for what you can control** - Rarely is your boss such a micro manager that there isn't room within their plans for you to maneuver and make it a success. Look for what you can control, the message, the action steps, the follow through. There are ways you can make almost any plan successful, your role is to find it. So look, then look again.
- **Take action** – Ideas are useless if they are not put into action. Inactivity, or just letting things happen, is letting your leadership atrophy.

There are plenty of leaders who are still around who have pushed the blame for failure down to their subordinates or blamed their boss or events "out of their control". But that strategy for career survival doesn't last forever, eventually you will be asked to produce results. Remember, it isn't what happens to you that matters, it's how you react to it.

LESSON ASSIGNMENT: Make a list of the people, processes and things that are inhibiting your ultimate success. Now next to that, write what aspect of this you control. And next to each of these write down what action you can take this week to deal with each of them.

Management is Easy, Just Always be Right

"Management is doing things right; leadership is doing the right things." ~Peter Drucker

"Successful people make the right decisions early and manage those decisions daily." ~John Maxwell

. . . . .

The title of this chapter is straightforward and I guess almost demoralizing depending on how you look at it, but that's not where I want to take it. This came to me during the course of a day where my decisions were being questioned more than usual. The reason we have all been chosen by our superiors to be in the role of a leader is because they felt we would make the right decisions. That doesn't mean that we will always make the right decisions, but whether from above (our boss) or below (our staff), that is often what we perceive the expectation to be. *Do not* let yourself fall into the trap of striving for perfection.

Perfection is an interesting and alluring goal, but typically results in inaction and demoralization. We should strive to make as many well thought out decisions as possible. These will not always be right, but our responsibility is to learn from these mistakes. Oftentimes we will make the right decision, but the result won't turn out well. These things happen. If you go back and look at how you made the decision and what factors went into it, then you are OK if you would have made the same decision over again. The greatest leaders are those who take action, make decisions, and learn from both the wrong decisions *and* the right decisions. If you take well thought out action and learn from success and failure, you will find that your decisions will be easier to make and right far more than they are wrong.

So don't fall into the perfection trap that seems to be the expectation for all of us. Focus on making decisions with the best information available and in a thoughtful way and see your "right decision percentage" increase with every decision you make.

LESSON ASSIGNMENT: A "perfect" leader is one who freely admits his mistakes and learns as much as possible from them. The next time you are haunted by your failure, remember that and get to learning.

New Thinking on Dressing for Success

"Know, first, who you are; and then adorn yourself accordingly." ~Epictetus

"Clothes make the man. Naked people have little or no influence in society." ~Mark Twain

"The clothes make the man" is *way* overstating the impact of clothing, but what I do agree with is that the clothes can handicap a person. Clothes are a tool of management, certainly not the most important, but one that should not be overlooked. Clothes can be an extension of body language and how you carry yourself. For good or bad, people will look to your clothing for clues on how they should treat you. Are you dressed better than them, the same, or worse? Depending on that perception, you may find yourself gaining or losing influence over them. So as a leader, how do you manage your dress for maximum benefit?

- **Who is the audience** – First and foremost you need to know who your audience is. If I have any meetings with my boss or his boss, you better believe I am dressing up. If it is a day of training my staff, it will be dialed back a notch…or even more depending on my intention.
- **What is your intention** – Do you want to make a statement that you are one of them? In a position greater than theirs? Or are you making a statement that you aren't afraid to get dirty in the trenches? Dressing different than everyone else isn't good or bad, it just depends on your intention.
  - Recently we were tasked with bringing more polish and professionalism to our guest interactions. What did I do? I started wearing ties every day and my suit jacket around the office more (buttoned oftentimes). It was a little thing that may have helped, but certainly couldn't hurt the effort. I was modeling the change we were looking for in the way employees engaged with guests.
  - A year prior to that I felt that there was too much separation between myself and the team so in addition to a number of other things I started matching their t-shirts and jeans that were worn on casual Friday.
  - The point is that it can be an evolution.
- **How do they dress** – Look for colors, patterns, cuff links, suit types (for men, number of buttons, for women, pants or skirts). Fashion in the magazines may be much different than fashion

within your organization, so look for the clues. In fact, I would almost ignore magazines and look internally.

Again, the value you bring to the organization is the most important thing, but clothes are a part of your toolbox and should be used to help your efforts to improve the operation. So do not neglect thinking on your clothing choices.

LESSON ASSIGNMENT: For one week set a calendar reminder at the end of your day to review who your audience will be on the next day. Then set your wardrobe based on that. The idea is to be "intentional" with your dress code.

Don't Just See What YOU Want to See

"However beautiful the strategy, you should occasionally look at the results." ~Winston Churchill

"Things don't change, only the way you look at them." ~Carlos Castaneda

"You can see a lot by looking" ~Yogi Berra

. . . . .

It's human nature to put blinders on and see the world the way we want to see it. By "want" I also mean the way we think a situation will work out, the way that is easiest for us, or any other sort of preconception. This is called "confirmation bias" and can have damaging effects on both our personal and professional lives because it skews our ability to see the world for how it truly is and guide our actions based on that reality.

One reason that "put yourself in your customer's shoes" is such a powerful saying is that most leaders are looking at things from the wrong point of view and find that they discover something after putting this saying into practice:

- The sales floor isn't laid out right?
  - It is confusing unless you work there.
- The employees aren't explaining the product well enough?
  - They are only passing along the basic information, which leads to quick transaction time, but an uninformed customer that could lead to dissatisfaction.
- We really don't have enough stock of this color?
  - As much as we want to cross sell into other colors (and think that we can), all they really want is the red one.

But beyond the obvious examples, we need to roll that process out to other areas we oversee so that we can anticipate and react to our business better. What you are looking for is the *brutal* reality. Reality in how your staff is performing, how your projects are progressing, how you are leading, etc. I recommend a simple test on your most important activities and performance metrics. Ask yourself these four questions when reviewing areas you oversee or traits you and your team should possess:

1. What would your boss find right or wrong?
2. What would *their* boss find right or wrong?
3. What would the customer find right or wrong?
4. What would your employees find right or wrong?

As I said, it is very natural and human to skew your viewpoint on things to fit personal motivations. The great leaders are able to see things from multiple angles, and thus get a better view on reality which leads to better decisions.

LESSON ASSIGNMENT: Take out a piece of paper and write down everything that is going wrong in your organization. Now ask yourself what about each of those issues is actually going well. Build personal and team momentum around what is going right to tackle what is going wrong. Now on the other side of that paper write down everything that is going right. In similar fashion to the above, ask yourself what is going wrong or could be made better with each of those items. Set to work addressing those to magnify their success. If you get stuck in either of these tasks, ask yourself the four questions above.

The Manager's Diary II

Projects

When All Eyes Are Watching

The Manager's Diary II

Plan to Fail

"Men meet with failure because of their lack of persistence in creating new plans to take the place of those which fail." ~Napolean Hill

"You always pass failure on the way to success." ~Mickey Rooney

· · · · ·

One of the most powerful bits of advice I have picked up in project management or just management in general is to "plan to fail". Now this seems counterintuitive and defeatist, but it isn't when put into practice in the manner which was suggested to me. While we want and plan for our initiatives, projects and processes to succeed wildly, that isn't always what happens. What we need to do is to plan our actions for "*if*" a particular failure occurs. Usually we know where there is the potential for things to go wrong and if we can already have our plan in place for that occurrence, it just becomes a part of the process. When we do this a few things happen for us:

- **Less demoralized** – Failure just becomes another step in eventual success, nothing to worry about because we already know what we are going to do because we knew if this didn't work we would do _____.
- **Quicker eventual success** – Since you have anticipated the series of events, you can quickly put your new plan into action. No brainstorming, second guessing, or other time

intensive things, just action. And action also fights any demoralization that crops up.
- **More control over your destiny** – When you plan to fail you take control over all events in your path which is an incredibly empowering thing (in fact, the definition of empowerment)

So how do you do it? You ask the three questions that the great project managers and great managers ask:

- **What are the most likely points of failure?** Don't obsess and look for failure in every nook and cranny, just come up with the top three to five likely failures. Any more than that and you are taking too much time from managing the present and likely future. These should be focused on the next steps along the path of the project, initiative or process.
- **What can you do/try when that occurs?** Come up with a quick, but reasonably complete, plan for dealing with the occurrence. Simple as that (OK, that isn't always simple).
- **Now that the original plan has changed, what can trip up progress?** With the new reality, you need to jump back up to the first question. Some of the three to five points may still be in play, but check to ensure you have the most likely points.

This makes failure a part of the plan. Your initiative and projects no longer become derailed, they simply take a different fork in the road, and doesn't that sound better and more empowering?

LESSON ASSIGNMENT: What are three failures that could occur this week (this week's Sale is a flop, everyone calls out sick, something important is delayed, etc). Now write them down on a piece of paper and write down your action plan if they occur. Next week write down the three biggest things that could go wrong and go through the same exercise....then ask yourself if you feel better about the week to come.

The First Feedback Can Be the Most Important

"Success or failure in business is caused more by the mental attitude even than by mental capacities." ~Walter Scott

"It is our attitude at the beginning of a difficult task which, more than anything else, will affect its successful outcome." ~W. James

. . . . .

Physics gives the best description of the title: Once something is at rest (has no feedback or no momentum in one direction or the other), a slight push in one direction requires a greater push in the other direction to change the momentum. So if you see something start out positive, you are inclined from that point forward to see things positively, likewise the same for things that start out negative.

So what to do? Well obviously, for yourself, you need to be aware of this tendency so that you see things for how they truly are. You need to ensure that you are taking the first data, the latest data, and all of the other data into account when making your assessment and not being swayed by the order it came in (by prior momentum). You need to ask yourself whether you are seeing things for what they truly are.

But what about everyone else? You may be aware of the bias towards the first data, but that doesn't mean you will be at all successful in explaining that to anyone else. So how do you manage this bias?

- **Set the expectation** – Let them know that you will review the data at regular intervals. That way they know that there are more reviews coming, not just what pops up first. They also know that whether positive or negative, there will be more data coming, so there is no concern that you are getting data to counteract other data.

- **Start out with a bang** – In a perfect world, you can structure the project or initiative to start out in the right direction, thus using this phenomenon for your benefit. If you can do this, then by all means, shout the success from the rooftops to leverage it to its full extent for all stakeholders. You may know ahead of time that a project will start out slow. In these cases you can build that into the expectations to create more success.

Another way to use this phenomenon is with your vendors or third party partners. If things start going bad, you can look to leverage that for concessions or extra work on their part to turn it around right from the beginning. The main thing though, is to realize that this phenomenon exists. Once you realize it, you can manage yourself and others better. And that's what we all strive to do.

LESSON ASSIGNMENT: Each day brings a new beginning. Focus on starting the day for your team on a positive note. Send out one of the inspirational quotes at the back of this book, tell everyone a joke, pass along a success from the day prior, or just about anything to give everyone a push in the right direction at the beginning of their day.

Flip-flopping Isn't Always Bad

"The most successful business people hold onto the old just as long as it's good & grab the new just as soon as it's better" ~Lee Iacocca

"The pessimist complains about the wind. The optimist expects it to change. The Leader adjusts the sails." -John C. Maxwell

· · · · ·

We talk a lot about perseverance because that is typically in far greater need than the alternative; changing your mind or changing direction. But realize that these are not necessarily bad things. The key is not to quit on the *goal*, but perhaps it is worth quitting on *how* you get to your goal. There is a time where it is appropriate to change your mind. The quote above from Lee Iacocca summarizes the ideal scenario perfectly where change is always done in the instant one option becomes better than another.

Being innovative is important and trying many things to reach your goal is important, but you won't always get it right. Now changing direction is not something to be taken lightly, it requires a loss of time and resources that were already spent on the other direction, and new vigor in re-launching momentum in the new direction. The questions to ask before changing course:

- **Why are you changing?** What exactly has failed? What results were you looking for? Basically make sure that you have your goals and metrics defined.

- **Is there a better option?** Instead of changing direction entirely, are there tweaks to the current model that make more sense? Have you explored all of the best options? Make sure you have learned as much as you can along the way so that you are better equipped to succeed in the future.
- **What data determines whether one option is better than another?** Is that a valid determiner of direction? It is incredibly important that you make your decisions based on data and not emotion, so look to the data behind your decisions. It also highlights the importance of the metrics.

The ability to recognize that your current direction is not going to get you to your goal is a crucial aspect of leadership. Perseverance should not equal stubbornness, when a change needs to be made, make it…..but ensure that you are doing so for the right reasons.

LESSON ASSIGNMENT: Take out any current projects you are working on that are struggling. Now come up with some alternatives to reaching the goal of each project. Do some of those alternatives look more promising than your current course of action? These are the ones that you need to look at a little more and apply the questions above.

Always Toughest Near the Mountaintop

"We do these things, not because they are easy, but because they are hard, because that goal will serve to organize and measure the best of our energies and skills." ~John F. Kennedy

"It is our attitude at the beginning of a difficult task which, more than anything else, will affect its successful outcome." -W. James

. . . . .

Things are always more difficult near the end of the journey. We've been at it for a long time and we are tired and just want it finished. This phenomenon crops up in a few areas of our work life:

- **The last days of a project** – The most common one we all face, where the excitement has worn off, we've tackled some issues as they've come up, but the end isn't quite in sight yet.
- **The 2nd or 3rd layers of process improvement** – You've already made the big improvements, now you are just "sharpening the saw" as Stephen Covey said. You're improving, but only in the scope of cents, not dollar. It's necessary and good, just not as exciting as the larger improvements.
- **The upper echelons of your career** – Opportunities for advancement are fewer and further between as you reach the top of the career ladder. Too often, people with potential lose some of their passion as the exciting next step is longer in coming.

The view from the top is great, but the air gets thin which makes each step harder. The satisfaction of completing your work is wonderful, but you'll likely be exhausted. There can only be so many groundbreaking improvements, but finishing strong is often the quality that separates good leaders from great leaders. So how do you do it?

- **Look how much you have done** – Don't look at how far you have to go, look at how far you have come. The sense of accomplishment reinforces that your time was productive and can give you a boost to try to do even more.
- **Work up a plan for the rest of the journey (you should already have one)** – Fight the unknown by having a plan. This allows you to create the short term wins that will keep you going, and who knows, once you write it down you may find there wasn't as much to do as you thought. Create milestones from this roadmap and focus on each successive one.
- **Find a point of personal motivation somewhere** – Whatever it may be for you; Bragging rights, commission dollars, proving someone wrong, etc. Visualize what it will be like when you are finished. Grasp for that motivation to finish strong.

A part of this is simply just knowing that it will get tough at the end of what you are working on. That's the reality. If you know you have an obstacle ahead it's easier to deal with it, it becomes something you expect and can prepare for. So know that it gets tougher at the top of the mountain, the end of a journey almost always is (and is always worth the effort).

LESSON ASSIGNMENT: The next project that you undertake, or whatever project you currently have, spend a few minutes integrating the above by including more milestones in the second half and clearly written result for how things will be afterward.

Don't Fall in Love with Your Plan

"Just because something doesn't do what you planned it to do doesn't mean it's useless." ~Thomas A. Edison

"It is a bad plan that admits of no modification." ~Publilius Syrus

. . . . .

Too often when we implement a plan, we are worried about striking a balance between persistence and stubbornness. This treats your plan as a fixed object as opposed to something that is adjustable and moveable. Put another way, your plan should always be in the "planning" stage. You make the original plan based on the best information available to you at the moment, but as you put a plan into action you get more information and new information. It's an evolutionary process.

Putting a plan into action is like driving through fog, we know what general direction we are going and the destination, but we can't see the whole path until we get right on top of it. Changes to a plan don't necessarily mean anything is wrong, there may just be opportunities that couldn't be seen at the beginning. Adjustments that take advantage of these opportunities are *very* good things and should be sought out.

One of the primary pieces of information we get is what's working and what isn't. These are your chances to double down (if something is working), or to send resources to areas that need assistance. Keeping organization resources in the areas where they do your organization the most good is essential to success in management.

Furthermore, you should be updating timelines and expected result as things grow clearer. This gives you a clearer idea of how to proceed. Have you gained time to completion because some things went smoother than anticipated? Should you spend that time on an enhancement? Does that free resources to assist in another area? Are the expected results shrinking or increasing? What impact does that have on project scope?

Expect changes to your plan, because a responsible leader will change the plan when there are better benefits to be gained. And quite frankly, there hasn't been a single plan in corporate history that went exactly as planned. This freedom, however, does not mean that you are free to delay completion continually. At a certain point you need to get something across the finish line, and that need should be balanced against the opportunities that arrive over the course of implementation.

LESSON ASSIGNMENT: There is an old military saying that "no battle plan survives the first bullet that is fired" and I want you to keep that in mind with any current projects you are managing or the next one that is put on your plate. Relax, adjust and win!

The Goal Isn't a Field Goal

"Our goal is a touchdown, not a bunch of field goals. Driving 99 yards down the field to only get a field goal is not a successfully executed plan." ~Cameron Morrissey

"Think little goals and expect little achievements. Think big goals and win big success." ~David Joseph Schwartz

It's important to celebrate success, but success can't be defined only as progress. In the quote above, you made it almost the entire length of the football field, but the goal isn't field goals. A baseball analogy may be that a triple is great, but if you don't get the runner across home plate, you didn't accomplish anything. While progress is important, it should never be treated in the same way as success. This comes about because we aren't clear about our goals. We don't want a situation where everybody feels like they won when they didn't (it might sound nice, but there needs to be a differentiation).

Acknowledge progress, but celebrate success!!!

Celebrating not reaching what you wanted to reach doesn't encourage your staff to reach further, it encourages them to cut corners and start looking for the "just enough." It also starts down the road to celebrating mediocrity. It serves a purpose to celebrate coming close to your goal, but never compromise what the goal actually is.

Now some of you may say "Well then we might not celebrate all of our hard work. Shouldn't that be celebrated?" I say that hard work should be acknowledged, but only reaching goals should be celebrated. This is why realistic goals, or at least realistic milestones need to be set. If you constantly reach too high, your risk your staff getting demoralized.

Celebrate what you want to see more of. While we like to see progress, what we really want to see is successful accomplishment of goals.

LESSON ASSIGNMENT: For any project that you are working on currently, come up with a plan for celebrating only when you reach milestones or when certain thresholds are met when it is implemented.

Overinvest in Early Wins

"Celebrate what you want to see more of." ~Tom Peters

"If you want more than one win, celebrate the first." ~Cameron Morrissey

. . . . .

It is vital to establish an expectation of excellence in your department, but when mediocrity has been the rule for so long, how do you turn it around? One of the most important things to do is set goals and succeed!

You must overinvest in early wins to show that success is possible, that it is fun, and that it is what you are in business to do. The first milestone reached, the smallest improvement, all should be celebrated so that you can build momentum in the right direction. First of all, you must start strong in anything that you do to last long enough to finish strong (build momentum early to make it through the tough times). But also, too often, staff and peers may not have enough personally at stake (or simply lack the pride) to spend the effort to push it through the inevitable difficulties. This is where celebrating success comes in.

So how do you communicate the success?

- **Let them know what they achieved** – But beyond just numbers, go one step further, and talk about the impact to the business in the biggest way possible:
  - 10 more loyal customers this week are each worth $500 in revenue every year (based on spending patterns). So those 10 are worth a total of $5,000 to the company. If we retain

10 more customers every week this year, that is worth $260,000 in extra revenue. What if we retain 20 per week, or 50, what impact would that have?
- **Let them know what the next step is** – Success is always a path, not a destination, so what will you be working on next? How you will be working on it? And what does success looks like? So in the example above: How can you retain 20 or 50 more?
- **Let them know that there is another reward** – People want to succeed, but they also like to see incentives. So throw them a party, let them wear jeans, and let them know that there are little things in it for them as well as the big things. So in the example: If we retain 20 next week I'll buy the team pizza. If we retain 10 a week for the next month everyone can leave an hour early.

By investing heavily, you will also get visibility into a few things:

- **Who wants to jump on the bandwagon** – Some of your staff may have sat on the sidelines, but people are naturally attracted to success, so you will find people wanting to join the initiative.
- **Who needs to hand off the baton (relay race)** – Others will get tired from the effort, or will have neglected other duties, and need to go back to those. These individuals are still on board, but have not found a lasting balance as of yet.
- **Who needs to get off the bus** – And lastly, some just aren't ready yet and need off the initiative. These individuals are the ones that will need to shape-up or ship-out and it is best to be able to address them early (and please realize that you *will* have some that don't want to get on the bus at all)

So invest as much as possible in turning the momentum in your favor from the start. Those little wins in the beginning turn into huge wins down the road. Once you have begun to change the culture to one of excellence it becomes a little easier to move it even further forward.

LESSON ASSIGNMENT: What goal or good thing was accomplished in the last week? Now publicize and celebrate it as laid out above. Make it a point to do this once a week for a month to get you into the habit.

Step Up Before Your Employees Step Down

The Manager's Diary II

Peers:

You're A Player Not Just a Coach

The Manager's Diary II

Beware of the Agreement Monster

"A good manager doesn't try to eliminate conflict; he tries to keep it from wasting the energies of his people. If you're the boss and your people fight you openly when they think that you are wrong - that's healthy." ~Robert Townsend

"Conflict is the gadfly of thought. It stirs us to observation and memory. It instigates to invention. It shocks us out of sheeplike passivity, and sets us at noting and contriving." ~John Dewey

. . . . .

Are meetings in your workplace going really smoothly lately? Is every idea "golden"? Is it getting to be a bit of a love fest around the office? While this may very well just be a great time to be employed with your organization, I would argue that everyone has begun to either fear conflict, or complacency has set in.

Conflict can and should be healthy in the workplace. Criticism is the crucible in which great ideas are purified, and often can lead to entirely new ideas. Voicing your concern over an idea or direction also engages your mind, helps you stay "present" throughout the discussion, keeps you focused on what is important, and keeps you fired up and energized through your day (nothing like a spirited debate to do that for you).

But before you launch into a debate competition instead of a meeting, your discussion needs to carry the following elements:

- **Trust** – This is the key step and the gateway to constructive criticism. Everyone needs to know that everyone else has the best interests of the organization or department at heart. This is no place to tread if you are worried about people settling scores or just looking out for themselves
- **Respectful (if passionate) Discourse** – Don't allow things to get too heated when discussing the topic. Stay issue focused, it is *not* personal.
- **Leave it in the Room** – Once you leave the meeting it is back to work, no hard feeling, and no baggage. Remember, it was just business and you were all working toward the same goal.
- **But Don't Leave the Decision There** – Make sure that you reach some sort of decision, even if it is to discuss further at a later time. You don't want to just let it die and everyone not know what was decided, you must be clear.

Healthy debate ensures only the best ideas survive. Even when you "lose" the argument you have often set the stage for improvements down the road. Your idea may not get put into action now, but perhaps next month it will. So make sure that if everyone is in agreement, they are in agreement for the right reasons. Debate and disagreement is essential to ferreting out the very best ideas within your department or organization.

LESSON ASSIGNMENT: Even in healthy organizations this is often difficult to get going. Your role is to encourage this and "stir the pot" by arguing both sides of the idea in meetings and e-mail chains. Eventually as you go back and forth on an issue yourself, you will attract teammates on one side or the other for support. You moderate and encourage debate from the inside of the argument, not as a moderator on the outside. Given time and experience things will begin taking a life of their own. Your role is to mend any fences while the process takes root.

Take Care of Those Who Take Care of You

"It is literally true that you can succeed best and quickest by helping others to succeed." ~Napoleon Hill

"You can have anything in the world you want if you'll just help enough other people get what they want." ~Zig Ziglar

. . . . .

I'm not one to do favors for the sake of reciprocity, but one thing that my upbringing has taught me is that you take care of the people who support you in your endeavors, your support staff if you will. Now while I learned this outside of the business arena, it is an *absolutely* applicable and essential attribute for great leaders.

Business is a team sport, and I like to think of it as a relay race. If I can make things easier for the leg of the race before me, and the leg of the race after me, then we all win.

- **The Sales Team** is out facing the customer; when they call and need things, can I turn that around quick enough so they can get back to the customer on the same day, because that speed will impress clients and help them sell?
- **The Warehouse Team** is always beholden to emergency/expedited orders that are unpredictable in timing and volume. Can I as a department head help prioritize further? As a Sales Rep, can I build in a buffer to shipping

dates when the customer isn't in a rush? Can I send people to help if they have downtime or work that isn't an emergency?
- **The Accounting Department** is buried at the end of every month. Can I ensure that my day to day and week to week paperwork doesn't build at the end of every month? Can I reschedule weekly meetings a day earlier or later? What other work can I shift to other times in the month?

The principle is something most of us were taught by the time we finished Kindergarten: Just help one another. As leaders, when we help in these ways:

- **We demonstrate a level of teamwork that goes beyond the typical interpretation in business** - Sadly, most teamwork initiatives are internal to the department. By going outside and helping departments that are further upstream or downstream in the process you demonstrate to your team and others how it is truly done.
- **We build operational efficiencies** - Similar to the relay race analogy. Departments helping other departments ensures that the most effective use of everyone's time is being used.
- **We build goodwill** - Now I don't mean to use as favors, I simply mean that the overall goodwill of the organization increases as teamwork increases. This raises the tide for all boats.
- **It feels good** – Serving others is always a higher form of satisfaction and fulfillment. And those are two things employees site in surveys over and over again that they are interested in receiving.

In business, when we help each other in the simple and courteous ways described above it is called *synergy*. While that term is a bit of a cliché buzzword, the ideas laid out above are the action items of synergy. So focus on helping the entire operation, it is good for the soul of the entire organization, is good for your career, and is just plain good business.

LESSON ASSIGNMENT: How can you make life easier for each department you touch? Make a list of the things you could do. Now choose one of these to put in place every week for the next month and watch what happens. I'm sure you'll be pleased.

Fresh Ideas from the Un-involved

"Don't cheat people of their growth. Empower them to solve problems and generate ideas. Watch them grow!" ~Stephen Covey

"The great leaders are like the best conductors - they reach beyond the notes to reach the magic in the players." ~Blaine Lee

. . . . .

Want a fresh perspective on things? Want some new ideas? Go talk to Accounting about your problems. If you need something new and fresh you will have to go where you haven't gone before. Marketing will always talk, Operations isn't usually too shy, but Accounting rarely is asked for insight and therefore will have the best chance to have a truly fresh idea you never thought of. Likewise there are people in your department (possibly more introverted) who represent an opportunity for new insight and ideas. These people sit quietly out of fear they may be wrong, possibly due to insecurity, or just don't feel you will value their opinion.

Unleashing ideas and giving a sense of personal power over the course of the business are two extraordinarily impactful things to focus on with team members. Most organizations allow the boisterous people and silos to run the business and neglect those with quieter voices or who are in different areas that don't obviously have a direct responsibility over direction and vision. This is an *enormous* missed opportunity.

A couple of points to drive forward the "Why" and "How" of this:

- **Explanation is often enlightening** - The process of explaining the issue in a way that other departments can understand often yields benefits for you along the way. You need to cut through the complexity for them to understand so you are forced to find simplicity in the issue. This also ensures that *you* understand the issue, as we too often are missing the solution within the problem through our own understanding.
- **No strings attached** – Idea creation suffers sometimes due to fear of blame, ownership, or a fear that it will just create extra work. If you rid your discussions of these three elements, you may unleash a torrent of ideas with just this. P.S. this works just as well for your staff as well.
- **Lays groundwork for future collaboration** – Silos are a dangerous thing in companies today, and any time you reach out to another department, you take a brick away from the wall between departments. This just makes it easier in the future to communicate more effectively, whether on ideas or on regular day to day activities.

So reach out to those who either don't have a voice or don't use their voice, you will find the experience informative, and possibly, *extremely* helpful!

LESSON ASSIGNMENT: Make a list of people who are open to discussions in other departments. These are the ones who have probably already given you their "two cents" on other issues. The next time you need a fresh perspective, look to this list.

How to Turn Defeat into Victory

"Men meet with failure because of their lack of persistence in creating new plans to take the place of those which fail." ~Napolean Hill

"Success or failure in business is caused more by the mental attitude even than by mental capacities. ~Walter Scott

. . . . .

At the moment you lose an argument or discussion point, ultimate defeat has not always been decided. You may have lost the battle, but the war may not have been decided. It all depends on what you learn and what action you take. Too often we take discussions of policy, projects and directions and turn them into defensible "Me vs. You" sort of discussions. This is short sighted and neglects a longer term opportunity for you and the organization.

Always remember you are there to serve the organization or department, not to just serve your ideas. I recommend three things when you lose an argument that lays out a direction or action items you were opposing:

- **Invite yourself to the after party** – Too often when we lose an argument we shut down, leave the room, and pass on complete ownership to the opposing party. *Don't.* Stay and be a part of the planning of the next steps. This proves that you are not a sore loser, that you have something to contribute, and are willing to do what is best for the organization/department.
- **Don't be a wallflower** – Be an advocate for the opposing idea's success (remember, the battle is over). Offer to be an active participant in some facet of the idea, don't just observe, pout, and withhold your services. Lending your expertise and abilities helps with overall success and gives you a stake in that success. A little success for you is better than none at all.
- **Be the life of the party** – Look for ways to improve the idea and take it to the next level. You are not looking to take over the idea (this isn't a coup), just make it as successful as possible. This is where you can showcase your talent and maturity. It also allows you to take some ownership of the direction you may have initially opposed.

You will win some and lose some, but the person who leverages the losses in a positive way will gain either way. When you set pride aside and move quickly from the failure of your argument to the success of the decision, you open up opportunities for you to shine and use your abilities. This is very uncommon in this day and age so it will make you stand out. Depending on how it goes, it could be an even bigger success for you down the road.

LESSON ASSIGNMENT: Get ready to say the following (very sincerely) the next time a course of action is decided on that wasn't your own…. "OK, that's cool, how can I help?"

Feeling Down or Un-empowered? Go Next Door

"When we can no longer change a situation, we are challenged to change ourselves." ~Viktor Frankl

"You can't live a perfect day without doing something for someone who will never be able to repay you." ~John Wooden

• • • • •

One of the most important things that you can learn as an employee, manager or business owner is how to pick yourself up when you are feeling down. It happens to all of us from time to time, it's just human nature. Sometimes it is work related, sometimes customer related, and sometimes you're just having a case of the "Mondays". Regardless of the reason, the quicker you regain your focus and drive, the better for everyone.

One of the ways I have learned to do that is to walk over to another department and help them with one of their tasks. I've created a spreadsheet, shared some of my SOPs, gave my opinion of a new design, and even unloaded boxes from a shipping container (OK, I only unloaded literally three boxes). This helps for a few reasons.

- Getting a change of scenery breaks the routines and ruts we find ourselves in on a daily basis, which can help us out of our "funk."
- It feels good to lend a hand and expertise in another area that may be lacking your talents. This gives us a kick of pride to get us moving on our own tasks.

- It is the right thing to do because it builds a sense of camaraderie and community within the organization. It also could lead to more collaboration in the future.
- With small tasks, you also get the feeling of accomplishment and success.

Now of course, you have your own department to run, so you can't take on responsibilities or large projects in other areas. But it is a nice way to add some spice to your day and give you a "pick me up" when you are feeling down. I encourage you to try it.

LESSON ASSIGNMENT: The first thing you need to do is to foster relationships in other departments. Start popping by occasionally and asking people how their day is going. It's friendly and polite, and it will also indicate to you which people are more open in their communication. From here you can start asking those people what they are working on. Do this for a little while and some of those individuals will start talking about their struggles and *that* is when you can begin putting your skills to use.

Be the Focused and Calming Influence

"Leadership is a matter of having people look at you and gain confidence in how you react. If you're in control, they're in control." ~Tom Landry

"When you build bridges, you can keep crossing them." ~Rick Pitino

Step Up Before Your Employees Step Down

The most important thing as a leader is ensuring that things get *done* and *done well*. One of the more common ways that this process gets delayed or completely derailed is when tensions escalate. Since the most important issues in any operation tend to be the ones people are most passionate about, this is relatively common in a meeting or collaboration setting. Your ability to drive the focus of the collaboration toward the resolution of the issue, even when tensions escalate, is essential.

Obviously you need to present a calm and productively focused demeanor yourself to be successful. Escalating tension by yourself will not serve you at all. But also one of the best ways to be the calming influence is to be there right from the start. Nipping any of the negativity or tension in the bud is *much* easier than trying to stop it after it has a head of steam behind it. Some common ways this takes place are:

- **Kitchen Sink** – People start talking about everything that touches the issue, without talking about the issue itself. One of the tried and true ways to address this is "OK, but let's get back on track here". Simple, but refocuses everyone.
- **Defensiveness** – The issue really centers around one person/area and everyone knows it. Reassure everyone that we are focused on addressing the issue, and we don't care about blame. Again, stay issue focused.
- **Wild Tangent** – All of a sudden the discussion starts talking about a small part of the issue, or something only loosely related. Similar to the kitchen sink, bring it back to topic, everyone already knows they're off on a tangent.
- **Disbelief** – Everyone talks about how shocked they are and goes through all of the past history of the issue, "How could this possibly get this bad?" I recommend a hearty "OK, well let's solve it once and for all" to combat this and get it back on track.

Your ability to be the person that keeps focus on getting the results in a way where there is no bad blood created will have a powerful impact on your career moving forward. Keeping discussions issue focused and calm, whether in meetings, conference calls, or e-mail chains, is essential in doing just that.

LESSON ASSIGNMENT: The common idea of the four situations above is losing focus on the issue and giving in to an emotional response. At the beginning of every meeting and conference call, write "Issue _____" and fill it in. As the meeting progresses, focus on those words. Underline them, circle them, put stars on either side, just keep focusing on the issue.

A Rising Tide Raises All Boats

"Example is not the main thing in influencing others. It is the only thing."
~Albert Schweitzer

"A leader leads by example not by force." *~Sun Tzu*

. . . . .

I talk a lot about improving your department and learning from others, but I thought of the saying above in relation to your ability as a leader of an exceptional department to raise the bar for your peers and *their* employees. When your department excels it shows the rest of the organization what is possible. In some instances you redefine what is possible.

One example I always think of in regards to this are world records in sports. I believe that Usain Bolt's World Records (for instance) have a "pulling" effect on the rest of the field where a "if he can do it, I can do it" mentality prevails. If your department is excelling, then every other department *knows* that it is possible. Basically, you have eliminated restrictions for everyone. Once someone does something, the excuses fall to the wayside.

There is also a natural want/need to impress your boss. So if your peers keep hearing about how well you are doing, the desire to receive that same praise will spur them on to that extra effort to join you in the exceptional ranks.

But what is your duty as the leader that sets the example:

- **Share how you did it** – If you created a training program, share it. If you created a tracking spreadsheet, share it. Write down all of the hurdles you came across, and share them. As the old saying goes, you will only get what you give, so *give* your peers a helping hand.
- **Learn from their journey** – And in an attempt to "get" right away, take personal ownership and look for lessons in what your peer is doing. Nobody gets everything right the first time, and you certainly didn't either. Your operation can learn from others and then improve further and continue the virtuous cycle.

REMEMBER: It's nice when your ship is rising, but it's more fun to bring some people along for the ride.

LESSON ASSIGNMENT: Is there anything that is "generally" believed by your peers to be impossible, but that you have a feeling can be accomplished? I'd be willing to bet there are at least a few things. Choose one and set out your plan, memorialize it, and get to work to show them the way.

The Manager's Diary II

The Customer:

The Reason You Have a Job

The Manager's Diary II

Find Competitive Advantage Anywhere You Can

"The absolute fundamental aim of business is to make money out of satisfying customers." ~John Egan

The golden rule for every business man is this: "Put yourself in your customer's place." ~Orison Swett Marden

· · · · ·

Finding and sustaining a competitive advantage is one of the central functions of any properly run organization. But that doesn't mean it doesn't often start at the departmental level. Warren Buffett famously looks primarily for durable competitive advantage in the businesses he invests in. And while "durable" is what we seek, *any* competitive advantage is useful in the short or long term. Oftentimes it is complementary to what we already are working on as a competitive advantage, like the below model of customer service:

Tony Hsieh, the CEO of Zappos, tells the story in his book "Delivering Happiness" of when he anonymously called his Customer Service line with a room full of conference attendees and asked where the nearest pizzeria was to the hotel he was staying at. After a couple of quizzical questions to ensure this WAS actually the request, the customer service rep provided him with three options within a couple of blocks.

Not a typical experience, or one you want repeated all of the time if you are paying the salary of the customer service rep (you are probably not running a 411 information line), but an exceptional example of customer focus. And the ideas don't need to be huge. Here's one I'd like to see at every restaurant, café, and coffee shop I go to: *Phone charging stations with adapters in place*....that alone could give me an excuse to stop off at a particular place for a smoothie or cup of coffee if I was running errands and low on juice.

Here's a few places to look:

- **First, how can you better serve the customer** – Even if it isn't in your specific area of expertise, what do they need? What is useful to them? How can you help make their life easier? This is your starting point to see what need your resources can fill, and highlights the value of obtaining customer feedback. One of the key questions to ask is what are your customer's "pain point", those things that cause irritation?

    Virgin Group just opened up their first hotel in Chicago and went straight for some of the biggest nuisances of a hotel experience. Their WiFi is free and the minibar is stocked full of goodies that are priced the same as in a grocery store. They have created a competitive advantage out of customer pain points at their competition.

- **What resources do you have** – Distribution expertise, manpower, equipment, products, skills, etc

    One of the things I have done over and over again in my personal career is offer the services of my staff to any large data entry or special project that comes up in my organization, regardless of whether it has anything to do with my department. As I run one of the largest departments in each of the companies I have been a part of I have scale, scale that I can use to help the organization move forward, and from a personal standpoint, gives me more exposure.

- **Now match them up** – Start by taking a customer need/want and seeing if there is a way for you to satisfy it, Some you will be able to, some you won't, some will be too expensive, some will take too much time, but if you have gathered your feedback and know your customer well enough, you should be able to find something.
- **Crazy uses for your product/service** – Don't forget to think outside the box for ideas, sometimes *way* outside the box. Are customers using your product for something completely random? Do they stop off somewhere else right before, or right after they visit you? Don't forget to get crazy.

Gaining any sort of competitive advantage can be vital to success and survival, not just for the organization, but for your career as well. So grab it wherever you can by keeping an eye out for opportunities to be more impactful on your organization and the customer.

LESSON ASSIGNMENT: For your particular department, ask yourself what three things your customer dislikes about their experience and what three things they want? Now see what you can do to eliminate those things they dislike and meet their wants.

Create Value for Sustained Success

"There are so many men who can figure costs, and so few who can measure values." ~Unknown

"Our belief was that if we kept putting great products in front of customers, they would continue to open their wallets." ~Steve Jobs

· · · · ·

A little while back Bank of America announced that they were raising certain fees on their customers. Now in this case, it wasn't that they were passing cost increases along to customers (which isn't fun, but isn't the worst sin in the world either). They weren't creating more value, bettering service levels or providing anything more. They were simply trying to squeeze as much out of each customer as possible.

Successful Businesses Create Value

Bank of America's move was a horrendously short sighted decision that only opened up the door for criticism and competitors. Even in a mature industry like banking, there are always competitors ready to pounce on your mistakes. The value proposition of your product or service must constantly be moving forward in order to stay ahead of the competition and keep your organization successful. But this is also something we can look to do in our own departments to really juice our performance.

When was the last time you asked yourself, "what is important to my customers?" Is it cost, is it service, is it add-ons? What can you tackle in your area that affects what is important to your customers?

- **Low Cost** – Not always something you have any control over, but if there are coupons or discounts available, it is always a nice surprise to offer those up to customers.

But the two that are definitely in your control are:

- **Service** – Nobody likes to wait, so you should cross train to tackle lines as much as possible. Nobody likes speaking with a sales person who doesn't know what they are talking about, so train more effectively. Is your staff polite? Make sure they understand the basics of etiquette. What little things can you do to make your service stand out? Walk them to their car? Follow up with a call a few days later to ensure they don't have any more questions? Manage your inventory better to have the choices that customers value? There are almost always a few things that you can do to elevate your level of service to create value.

- **Add-ons** – Your organization most likely already has a program for this, but it is a wonderful way to create more value, especially if you can bundle things together like travel companies and provide a small discount. I saw this recently at Best Buy when looking at cameras, they had bundles that included cases, lenses, memory storage and batteries that came with a nice, but not extravagant discount. That's a great value, and a great reason to take my business there. Is there anything else you can add on to your product/service that has little or no cost to you that creates value?

The way to sustainably improve top-line revenue is to continue to create more and more value for your customers. It doesn't always need to be a big thing, oftentimes it can be a series of little things and it often starts at the department level. What can you improve easily and simply? Focus on value.

LESSON ASSIGNMENT: This week start with your three biggest customer complaints. Some may be out of your control, but you can surely influence some of them. Look for ways to solve or mitigate the negative effects of the issues. Next week it is time to move onto your opportunities. What three things could you do that would enhance the customer experience? Really look for things that would "wow" them. What can you do to get these things into effect?

Focus on Things That Won't Change

"Things don't change, only the way you look at them." ~Carlos Castaneda

"Face reality as it is, not as it was or as you wish it to be." ~Jack Welch

• • • • •

Amazon.com is a great example of a company focusing on the things constantly on the mind of their customers. Whether they are selling lipstick, tractor seats, e-book readers or data storage, it is all part of one big plan with three big constants: *offer wider selection, lower prices and fast, reliable delivery*. Those last three things are the things that customers will always want, and things that won't change. When you stay focused on the things that don't change in your own operation, you drive your employees' focus, and you never waste you efforts on the "flavor of the month".

So what might it be in your operation? Some possibilities:

- Friendly Customer Service
- Great Product Knowledge
- Impeccable Execution of Procedures
- Product Innovation

When you focus on the "constants" and try to improve them, you are aligning yourself with the customer. eBook readers allow for lower prices, the quickest delivery possible, and by cutting out the barriers to publishing, greater selection (independent authors have flourished). That's hitting *all* of Amazon.com's "constants", and is why eBooks are so successful *and* why Amazon.com has focused so intently on them.

In your world, finding ways to improve your "constants" can reap the same rewards. More product knowledge leads to better customer service, and with everyone understanding the product better, possibly significantly better product innovation. So find out what matters to your customers and what aligns with your business and set about focusing on improving those things that never change. You'll see a much more productive use of your time.

LESSON ASSIGNMENT: What one, two or three things can you focus the entire organization around? Remember that these are customer focused things as listed above, not organization focused things like sales or profit. Once you have these items listed start focusing on how you can enhance them from where they are now.

The Manager's Diary II

APPENDIX

Top Leadership & Management Quotes #101 - #200

Top 100 in "The Manager's Diary I: Thinking Outside The Cubicle"

. . . . .

101. "You can have anything in the world you want if you'll just help enough other people get what they want." ~Zig Ziglar
102. "When you have exhausted all possibilities, remember this: You haven't." ~Thomas Edison
103. "A clear vision, backed by definite plans, gives you a tremendous feeling of confidence and personal power." ~Brian Tracy
104. "Never wrestle with pigs. You both get dirty and the pig likes it." ~George Bernard Shaw
105. "First-rate people hire first-rate people; second-rate people hire third-rate people." ~Leo Rosten
106. "No one has ever made himself great by showing how small someone else is." ~Irvin Himmel
107. "Start by doing what is necessary, then do what is possible, and suddenly you are doing the impossible." ~St. Francis of Assisi
108. "Leaders keep their eyes on the horizon, not just on the bottom line." ~Warren G. Bennis
109. "My responsibility is leadership, and the minute I get negative, that is going to have an influence on my team." ~Don Shula
110. "Nothing will ever be attempted if all possible objections must first be overcome." ~Samuel Johnson
111. "Perfection isn't attainable, but if we chase perfection we can catch excellence." ~Vince Lombardi
112. "The measure of success isn't if you have a tough problem, but whether it's the same one you had last year." ~J.F. Dulles

113. "The most successful business people hold onto the old just as long as it's good & grab the new just as soon as it's better" ~Lee Iacocca
114. "The only real mistake is the one from which we learn nothing." ~John Powell
115. "Losers quit when they're tired. Winners quit when they've won." ~Unknown
116. "Never tell me the sky's the limit when there are footprints on the moon." ~Anonymous
117. "To achieve greatness, start where you are, use what you have, do what you can." ~Arthur Ashe
118. "Effective leadership is not about making speeches or being liked; leadership is defined by results not attributes." ~Peter Drucker
119. "The greatest enemy of knowledge is not ignorance, it is the illusion of knowledge." - Stephen Hawking
120. "It is amazing what you can accomplish if you do not care who gets the credit." - Harry S Truman
121. "The whale is endangered, while the ant continues to do just fine." ~Bill Vaughn
122. "Try, try, try, and keep on trying is the rule that must be followed to become an expert in anything."~W.Clement Stone
123. "Never discourage anyone.....who continually makes progress, no matter how slow." ~Plato
124. "Hold yourself responsible for a higher standard than anybody expects of you. Never excuse yourself." ~Henry Ward Beecher
125. "It's not that I'm so smart, it's just that I stay with problems longer." - Albert Einstein
126. "Imagination is more important than knowledge." ~Albert Einstein
127. "The discipline of writing something down is the first step toward making it happen. " ~Lee Iacocca
128. "Action may not always bring happiness; but there is no happiness without action." ~Benjamin Disraeli

129. "Don't cheat people of their growth. Empower them to solve problems and generate ideas. Watch them grow!" ~Stephen Covey
130. "It is literally true that you can succeed best and quickest by helping others to succeed." ~Napoleon Hill
131. "A real leader faces the music, even when he doesn't like the tune." - Author Unknown
132. "Leadership, like swimming, cannot be learned by reading about it." ~ Henry Mintzberg
133. "Make sure your worst enemy doesn't live between your own two ears." ~Laird Hamilton
134. "A good objective of leadership is to help those who are doing poorly to do well and those who are doing well to do even better." ~Jim Rohn
135. "You may never know what results come of your actions, but if you do nothing, there will be no results." ~Mahatma Gandhi
136. "Most great people have attained their greatest success just one step beyond their greatest failure." ~Napoleon Hill
137. "You cannot change your destination overnight, but you can change your direction overnight." ~ Jim Rohn
138. "A leader is not an administrator who loves to run others, but one who carries water for his people so that they can get on with their jobs"
139. "A leader leads by example not by force." ~Sun Tzu
140. "Every time you share your vision, you strengthen your own subconscious belief that you can achieve it." ~Jack Canfield
141. "One machine can do the work of fifty ordinary men. No machine can do the work of one extraordinary man." ~Elbert Hubbard
142. To be a leader, you have to make people want to follow you, and nobody wants to follow someone who doesn't know where he is going. ~Joe Namath
143. "Be a yardstick of quality. Some people aren't used to an environment where excellence is expected." ~Steve Jobs

144. "A wise man can learn more from a foolish question than a fool can learn from a wise answer." ~Bruce Lee
145. "Lots of people want to ride with you in the limo, but what you want is someone who will take the bus when the limo breaks down." ~Oprah Winfrey
146. "A competent leader can get efficient service from poor troops, while an incapable leader can demoralize the best of troops." ~John Pershing
147. "Business is a continual dealing with the future; it is a continual calculation, an instinctive exercise in foresight." ~Henry R. Luce
148. "You must have long range goals to keep you from being frustrated by short range failures." ~Charles C. Noble
149. "A desk is a dangerous place from which to view the world." ~John Le Caré
150. "Anticipate the difficult by managing the easy." ~Lao Tsu
151. "Be decisive. A wrong decision is generally less disastrous than indecision." ~Bernhard Langer
152. "By failing to prepare, you are preparing to fail." ~Benjamin Franklin
153. "By stretching yourself beyond your perceived level of confidence you accelerate your development of competence." ~Michael Gelb
154. "Danger for most of us lies not in setting our aim too high & falling short; but in setting our aim too low & achieving our mark." ~Michaelangelo
155. "Deal with the world the way it is, not the way you wish it was." ~John Chambers
156. "Difficulties increase the nearer we approach the goal." ~Goethe
157. "Do not bring me your successes; they weaken me. Bring me your problems; they strengthen me." ~Anonymous
158. "Either you deal with what is the reality or you can be sure that the reality is going to deal with you." ~Alex Haley
159. "Every exit is an entry somewhere else." ~Tom Stoppard

160. "For success, attitude is equally as important as ability." ~Harry F. Banks
161. "Get the facts, or the facts will get you." ~Thomas Fuller
162. "Goals are like stepping-stones to the stars. They should never be used to put a ceiling or a limit on achievement." ~Denis Waitley
163. "Gold medals aren't really made of gold. They're made of sweat, determination, & a hard-to-find alloy called guts." ~Dan Gable
164. "I have been up against tough competition all my life. I wouldn't know how to get along without it." ~Walt Disney
165. "If timing ain't everything, it's damn close" ~Tom Peters #management
166. "If you are going to be a champion, you must be willing to pay a greater price." ~Bud Wilkinson
167. "If you do the work you get rewarded. There are no shortcuts in life." ~Michael Jordan
168. "If you don't like how things are, change it! You're not a tree." ~Jim Rohn
169. "If you have accomplished all that you have planned for yourself, you have not planned enough." ~Meddigo Message
170. "It is a bad plan that admits of no modification." ~Publilius Syrus
171. "It is better to look ahead & prepare than to look back & regret." ~Jackie Joyner-Kersee
172. "It is easier to do a job right than to explain why you didn't." ~Martina Navratilova
173. "It's never crowded along the extra mile" ~Wayne Dyer #management
174. "Just because something is easy to measure doesn't mean it's important." ~Seth Godin
175. "Kites rise highest against the wind - not with it." ~Winston Churchill
176. "Let a man lose everything else in the world but his enthusiasm and he will come through again to success." ~H. W. Arnold

177. "Look for people who will aim for the remarkable, who will not settle for the routine." ~David Ogilvy
178. "Make the present good, and the past will take care of itself." ~Knute Rockne
179. "Many of life's failures are people who did not realize how close they were to success when they gave up." ~Thomas Edison
180. "Mobilize resources to understand and satisfy the customer. That's business. If you're doing anything else, change direction"~Ben Acheson
181. "My troubles and obstacles, have strengthened me... a kick in the teeth may be the best thing in the world for you." ~Walt Disney
182. "Negativity breeds negativity. The wise focus on the positive in every person and every situation." ~Philip Arnold
183. "Never forget to maintain stability while advancing, and never forget to advance while maintaining stability." ~Li Ka-Shing
184. "No person was ever honored for what he received. Honor has been the reward for what he gave." ~Calvin Coolidge
185. "Nothing is so potent as the silent influence of a good example" ~James Kent
186. "Some men see things as they are and ask why. Others dream things that never were and ask why not." ~George Bernard Shaw.
187. "Success is the good fortune that comes from aspiration, desperation, perspiration and inspiration." ~Evan Esar
188. "Take the first step in faith. You don't have to see the whole staircase, just take the first step." ~Martin Luther King Jr.
189. "The difference between the impossible and the possible lies in a man's determination." ~Tommy Lasorda
190. "The first step towards getting somewhere is to decide that you are not going to stay where you are." ~JP Morgan
191. "The greatest waste in the world is the difference between what we are and what we could become." ~Ben Herbster
192. "The most rewarding things you do in life are often the ones that look like they cannot be done. " ~Arnold Palmer

193. "The triumph can't be had without the struggle." ~Wilma Rudolph
194. "The trouble with most of us is that we would rather be ruined by praise than saved by criticism." ~Norman Peale
195. "Unless you try to do something beyond what you have already mastered, you will never grow." ~Ralph Waldo Emerson
196. "What is not started today is never finished tomorrow." ~Johann Wolfgang von Goethe
197. "When you have a number of disagreeable duties to perform, always do the most disagreeable first." ~Josiah Quincy
198. "Whenever you do a thing, act as if all the world were watching." ~Thomas Jefferson
199. "You accomplish victory step by step, not by leaps and bounds." ~Lyn St. James
200. "You can't build a reputation on what you are going to do." ~Henry Ford

The Manager's Diary II

Epilogue

Well here we are at the end of this journey. So what should you do now? Leadership and management are deep subjects so there are many options available to us. The important thing as I see it is to keep learning and start another journey. Perhaps that is another one of my books, perhaps some books from The Manager's Diary Book Club, perhaps joining me on Facebook or Twitter, or maybe it is starting this book over again and seeing what else can be learned. Just know that there is no "end" to learning in leadership and management, you never get it all right, there is always something new to learn, and you will continue to be humbled by your own mistakes and the responsibility afforded you. So keep marching forward and enjoy the ride.

The Manager's Diary II

Made in the USA
Lexington, KY
03 September 2015